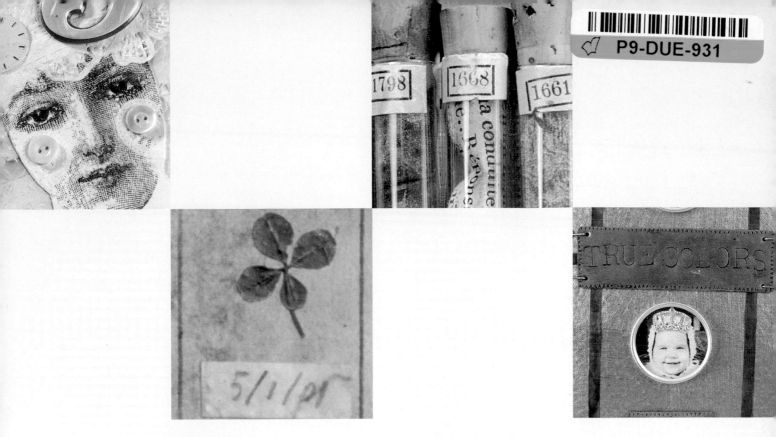

True Colors

A Palette of Collaborative Art Journals

Stampington & Company®

Laguna Hills, California

A Letter from the Publisher

Dear Reader,

In 2001, I received a call from Michelle Ward telling me that she and 14 other artists were working on a project involving the exchange of art journals. The artists offered to share the journals with us, and I was confident we were going to see an impressive collaboration. Still, I had no idea that we would witness an event that would "raise the bar" in the world of art journaling and capture the attention of anyone interested in altered art and mixed media.

The names of the participants alone should have given me some idea of the caliber of art we would be seeing, for these women are the divas of our industry. All are talented artists who would blush at this title and deny that they have taken art journaling to a new level, but take us, they have—on a journey where few have tread. They have opened the door for artists and crafters who may never have entered this realm had it not been for the passion-on-paper these color queens have shared with us.

Publishing the work of these women was both a privilege and a milestone in our company's history. The faith the artists placed in my team and me when they packed up their creations and entrusted them to our care was humbling, and I thank them for their confidence. From the moment we first saw these breathtaking journals to the day they were printed and bound in this special volume, we've enjoyed an adventure few publishers have had the opportunity to experience. The editorial and production team involved in creating *True Colors* has spent thousands of hours capturing the spirit of this collaboration. I'd like to thank them for their dedication and hard work.

I hope you enjoy your journey as you wander through these pages of imagination. More importantly, I hope this book inspires you to begin your own colorful excursion into the world of art journaling.

Kellene Giloff
Publisher

Publisher
KELLENE GILOFF

Editor
KATHRYN BOLD

Special Projects Editor
LINDA BLINN

Art Director
SONIA MARA ADAME

Graphic Designer
NANCY OH

Production Artist
TAWNY PHAM

Photo Stylist
EDA FARINACCI-
NYBERG

Photographers
SYLVIA BISSONNETTE
J.D. GIBBS
MELODY NUÑEZ

True Colors

A Palette of Collaborative Art Journals

Published in the United States
by Somerset Studio®
A division of Stampington & Company
22992 Mill Creek, Suite B
Laguna Hills, California 92653
949.380.7318

Prepress by Baseline Imaging, Monrovia, CA
Manufactured by Banta Book Group, Menasha, WI

First Edition 2003

ISBN 0-9717296-3-8

PHOTO CREDITS
Sylvia Bissonnette: 3-7, 8, 11, 14, 18-19, 24-25, 29, 32-33, 40-41, 43, 47, 49, 57-59, 63, 65, 75, 77, 79, 82, 88-89, 91, 94, 97, 99, 102, 107, 110-111, 116-117, 122-123, 125, 127, 131, 136-137, 141, 144-145, 148-151, 157, 165, 167, 168-169, 171, 174-175, 178-179, 182-183, 185, 187, 191, 194, 197, 199, 202-203, 205, 211, 213, 216-217, 220-221, 224-225, 228-229, 231, 235, 238-239, 242-243, 247, 252-253, 254-255, 258-259, 262-279.

J.D. Gibbs Photography: 3-7, 11, 13, 15-17, 20-23, 26-27, 29, 31, 34-39, 42, 44-45, 47, 50-56, 60-61, 63, 66-74, 77, 80-81, 83-87, 91, 93, 95-96, 98, 100-101, 103-105, 107, 109, 111-115, 118-121, 125, 128-129,132-135, 138-139, 141, 143, 146, 152-155, 157, 160-164, 166, 171, 173, 176-177, 180-181, 184, 187, 189-190, 192-193, 195-196, 199, 201, 204, 206-210, 213, 215, 218-219, 222-223, 226-227, 231, 233-234, 236-237, 240-241, 244-245, 247, 249-251, 253, 256-257, 260-261, 262-279.

Melody Nuñez: 3-9, 11, 13, 29, 33, 35, 44-45, 47, 56, 61, 63, 71, 77, 80, 91, 93, 96, 107, 109, 119, 125, 141, 143, 147, 155, 159, 171, 173, 187, 199, 204, 207, 213, 231, 233, 247, 262-279.

True Colors

A Palette of Collaborative Art Journals

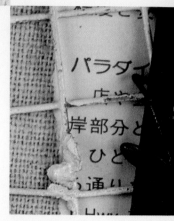

Traveling

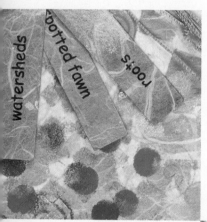

the Spectrum

An Exploration of Emotions, Hues & Mediums

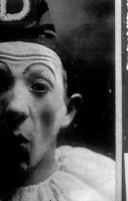

"I had forgotten what mustard fields looked like ... sheet upon sheet of blazing yellow, halfway between sulphur and celandine, with hot golden sunshine pouring down upon them out of a dazzling June sky. It thrilled me like music."

—Monica Baldwin, *I Leap Over The Wall (1950)*

Has color ever made you feel like that? Me, too.

I use my art journals to decode my impressions, impulses and inspirations. Color is my "way in," the most favored tool in my arsenal. One Saturday morning, in spring 2001, I got the idea to gather a group of journal artists together to explore the significance of color in our lives. I suspected these artists had an equal regard and appreciation for the topic and would relish an opportunity to express and share their observations. Each artist was invited to select a color and decide upon a format for her journal. As color selections were made, ("Sign me up for Black," or, "Red, please!") some offbeat color groupings also emerged, among them: Forest Floor and Sunset. The game was afoot.

The artists searched for their journals-of-choice, and some unexpected volumes entered the fray, including altered books and a vintage postcard album. The plan was for each artist to "set the tone" by creating the book covers, plus some introductory pages, then the journal would travel through a routing list, getting submissions from all 15 artists in our group. The project, which we called *True Colors*, lived up to its name.

by Lynne Perrella
Project Organizer

No matter where our ideas and inspirations came from, we all used color as a common language to express ourselves, yet each artist spoke in a voice that was uniquely hers. Our pages ran the gamut from childlike exuberance to austere sobering visions—a reminder that color provides a stage to express all emotions, dark to light. Entries recalled a clouded memory or paid enthusiastic homage to a beloved artist, lyric, or poem. Surprising elements, such as a recipe for black cake and music CDs with tunes that related to the color scheme, started to show up in the books. Online discussions raged throughout the project, covering lots of territory both artistic and personal. Lasting just over a year, *True Colors* provided strong cement for a group of artists and friends and resulted in a startling array of more than 500 journal pages.

As the project concluded, I realized that I was ready (if not eager!) to begin again. I had learned how truly bottomless the subject of color was, and I wanted to continue the celebration and investigation of it. Most of all, I knew how much I would miss the anticipation of receiving yet another of the journals in the mail and eagerly plotting my pages in the book at hand. Doing this book with Stampington & Company® has allowed all of the artists to revisit the many rewards of the project and tell our story. From subtle white to eternal black, and every color in between, we have taken a rich journey, singing the praises of color, all the way home.

ABOUT THE
True Colors
EXPERIMENT

True Colors began in May 2001 when Lynne Perrella of Ancram, New York, invited 14 artists from across the U.S. to participate in an unusual journal experiment.

Each woman was asked to begin an art journal based on a single color scheme. Being artists, they defined color their way. A few couldn't limit themselves to just one hue, so they picked two: Linn C. Jacobs opted for the unusual combination of Yellowgreen & Copper, while Teesha Moore's choice of Pink & Orange was arguably the most outrageous of the project. Several picked a color concept, such as Sunset or Autumn.

The artists' choice of journal was often unorthodox as well. Nina Bagley converted an old postcard album into her Metallics journal. The Yellowgreen & Copper journal isn't an album at all, but individual pages wrapped in fabric and tied up with ribbons—a gift of art. Anne Bagby created three books-in-a-box for her Violet & Yellow journal. One artist, Lisa Hoffman, ended up creating two journals, Aqua and Forest Floor, because the latter was temporarily missing in action. Once they decided upon a journal format, the artists decorated the books' covers using all kinds of mediums and found objects, from plastic paintbrushes to old optometrist lenses. For her Sepia journal, Judi Riesch adorned the cover of an antique leather book with tiny glass vials that contained paint or bits of paper in sepia tones.

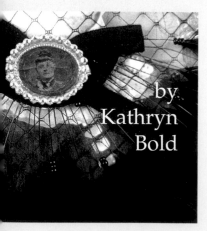

by Kathryn Bold

After completing several pages in their own journals, the artists mailed the books to each other according to a pre-arranged list. To keep the project moving, they had just two weeks to work on each a journal before sending it on its way. They felt nervous about entrusting such irreplaceable cargo to the mail, but that's the nature of a round-robin project. It's about trust, not only in the other artists, but also in the postal service. For 16 months, the journals circulated around the country, from Ancram, New York, to Anaheim, California, and points in between.

"I am not at all sure I can tell you in words how completely exhilarating it was working with this amazing group of women," Linn writes, in her essay about the Yellowgreen & Copper journal. "I felt so energized and so challenged. The fact that they live all over the United States was intriguing in itself. Think about it: 16 journals traveling back and forth, back and forth across the continent. In the back of my mind, I was always aware of where the originator lived and curious about what subtle influences that might have on the work, maybe in colors, textures or content."

The artists were free to use any medium they wished, and they did. The journals are filled with painting, sketching, metal work, embroidery, stamping, quilting—a great, colorful kaleidoscope of techniques and materials. Their entries range in theme and content from playful and exuberant to contemplative and even somber (the journals were in circulation on September 11, 2001, the day of the terrorist attacks on the World Trade Center and Pentagon).

"Because a theme such as color is broad and almost free of boundaries, it left plenty of room for artistic interpretation," Lisa Renner writes, in her essay for Blue & Ochre. "Each color evoked diverse emotions, and as each journal arrived, it was met with a new challenge and a new approach, resulting in unique creative resolve."

Over the course of the project, the journals grew heavy with twigs, buttons, milagros, foldouts, fabric, wire, and assorted ephemera. Michelle Ward's page in the Metallics journal even has a full-sized brass doorknocker. Michelle also gave the journals the gift of sound, creating CDs for each book with tunes that played on the color scheme.

For Keely Barham's Black journal, she compiled a little "Blackground" music that included a recording of "That Old Black Magic" by another Keely— Keely Smith. The journals became a full-sensory experience. They offered aromatherapy, in the form of incense, vanilla sticks and other scented additions from the artists. Karen Michel tucked incense into Linn's Yellowgreen & Copper journal because it struck her as "earthy." Many of the journals were intended to be touched. The velvet-covered Black journal was so cushy, Claudine Hellmuth had a hard time keeping her cat from curling up on top of it. Even the sense of taste came into play—Linn included a recipe from Gourmet for black cake in the Black journal, and the paper doughnuts Lynne made for Teesha's Pink & Orange journal looked good enough to eat.

Small wonder that the arrival of each journal in an artist's home or studio became a cause for celebration. Many savored the unveiling of the latest delivery, even creating small rituals to welcome the journals. As Judi put it in her introduction to the Sepia journal, "Each book's arrival was truly an event. Occasionally I would tear open the box before the postman drove away, but more often than not I would wait until later, using the unveiling as a treat or incentive to stay on task during the day. With coffee or wine in hand, I would savor each and every detail. I loved how the journals gradually began looking so full—they spilled out of all sides with ribbons, fibers, charms, beads, even mini CDs ala Michelle. The overflow was just a preview of the incredible details within."

Fear also greeted the journals on occasion. Most artists admit there was some aspect of the project that scared them silly. Claudine admitted she had to overcome her fear of "ruining" a journal. Sometimes they would experiment with a new technique, and realize—too late— that they certainly weren't going to try that again. Teesha, who often serves as her sternest critic, played with beeswax in the Forest Floor journal and described the results as an "experiment gone bad." She had better luck, however, in the Violet & Green journal when she tried coloring on fabric; she was so pleased with the results she surprised even herself.

While working on the journals, each artist had to weigh her own creative vision against those of the group. For artists who are notorious for their independence, this was no easy balancing act. "It was difficult not to be swept up into what other people had done," Linn writes. Yet the artists also saw the project as an opportunity to stray outside of their comfort zone and try new techniques, colors and materials. Sometimes they reveled in a newly acquired skill, and other times they realized that they'd rather create pages using a tried-and-true medium. Keely, for instance, started the project by working in

paper arts. After the first few journals, however, she switched to her preferred medium, fabric, because she wanted her entries to reflect her best work. It was the right call. Although she did wonderful things with paper, her fabric entries shine. As Karen writes in her statement on the Violet & Green journal: "Each journal truly emanated the spirit and style of the artist who made it, and at first it was quite a challenge to hold strong to my own vision and what I conceived to be my personal style. Working with the spirit of collaboration, I eased myself into the mingling of visions and images, getting my feet wet at first, then diving right into what turned out to be a very animated conversation of colors. I would listen closely to hear and feel what the book was saying to me and do my best as an interpreter."

During the project, the artists learned about themselves and each other. A constant stream of e-mail exchanges brought the group closer. Those who once knew each other by name only now felt a strong connection— bonded by colors. The 15 artists became a kind of sisterhood. In Lisa Hoffman's words, "With the frequent e-mail communications, it was obvious that we were weaving relationships as well as collaborations. I feel as though we all have a new and valuable network of friends who are there for us with the click of a computer key."

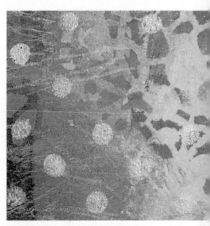

After the project ended in September 2002, each artist received her original journal—now crammed with colorful contributions. Most of the books had fibers, tags and charms dangling from their spines and pages. The Violet & Yellow journals came bundled up in tulle and confetti—a party in a box. The artists went online to share in the excitement of receiving their completed journals. Judi was overwhelmed when she saw her finished Sepia journal: "Each and every page, each and every woman, a gift," she writes.

In an e-mail to the group, Lynne likened the *True Colors* project to a party: "Sort of like Mardi Gras, where there are daytime parades, and nighttime reveleries, and pauses for banquets, and full-dress balls, and promendades—but it's ALL Mardi Gras."

The party's not over. Reluctant for the fun to end, the artists decided to share their journals with the public. They sent them off to Stampington & Company in Laguna Hills, California, to be photographed and shown in this book. *True Colors* is a party, all right, and now everyone's invited.

Who would have thought white could come in so many colors? Even the *True Colors* artists were surprised when they saw all of the shades used in the White journal, from pale ecru to pure, snowy white.

Lynne Perrella, organizer of *True Colors*, chose white for her journal because she figured the artists would be challenged by her pick. In fact, a few artists who were accustomed to using a lot of color admitted that they feared working in the White journal the most—until they saw what the others had done with their pages. White proved full of possibilities, and the journal ended up inspiring some of the artists' best creations.

White brought out the reflective side of the artists. Many found themselves thinking about the past and loved ones who had gone before them. They remembered ancestors with bits of linen and lace. Anne Bagby and Karen Michel both worked on the journal shortly after the terrorist attacks on the United States on Sept. 11th, 2001. Ann decided to create an entry in remembrance of her mother, who died "a quiet death" at age 89. Karen's page features a dove of peace—in white, of course.

Other artists (notably Judi Riesch) recalled weddings, First Holy Communions and graduation days. As the journal illustrates, white is a color of healing, a color of ritual.

Ermine muffs and old lace.
Sand dollars, seashells
and birch bark.
White on white—
as glorious as
the first snow in winter.

ORIGINATING ARTIST:
Lynne Perrella

I chose white because I knew I would be challenged and surprised by the color, and I hoped that the other artists would react in the same way. A favorite quote by cubist painter Juan Gris, "You are lost the instant you know what the result will be," came floating back to me, and I sensed that a whole journal of white, done by many artists, would be a treasure beyond measure. I was right. There is a quiet stillness about white, yet it can erupt in a snowstorm flurry of pattern and shifting light. It can bathe a page in a startling spotlight of intensity, or curl up in a quiet nest of calm. It seems to bridge all cultures, all time frames, all belief systems, and all seasons. It's a chalk line, or a snowy ridge, or a contrail from a jet, or an earthenware bowl of eggs, or an old letter. Of all the colors, it seems to have the most confidence, the most willingness to be itself in all its complicated-yet-simple glory. In a sense, white just is.
***

I started prowling around looking for the right journal, sure that I wanted a good generous-sized page, plus a spiral binding that would allow the artists to open the book flat and really explore the page surfaces. For the inside front and back covers, I created a grid of multiple swatches of white, running the gamut from winter-white to buff. When I had completed the work on the covers, I realized it was time to set the stage for the book by including something that was highly personal and carried special significance. My own photographs of an early-morning Ancram snowstorm provided the answer. The photos gave each artist a look at the view outside my studio door and provided a sense of the beauty and calm of the Hudson River Valley. I tucked one or two of the original photos into the mailing carton, hoping that someone would use them in her pages, and Michelle obliged with her lovely edelweiss entry. The journal that began here in Upstate New York eventually traveled to towns all over the United States, and came back to me as a testament to the quiet, shimmering passion of white.

—Lynne Perrella

WHITE

whitewash (hwīt'wŏsh), n. a composi-

whitewood (hwīt'wood), n. tulip-tree

white-smith (hwīt'smith), n. a tin-

or whiten (hwīt'en), v.t. to make white.

Also white-throat (hwīt'thrōt), n. a small

y small cake, on w
" were beautifully m
at it," said Alice, '
ger, I can reach th
row smaller, I can
er way I'll get into

48981

pure; innocent; having silvery hair;
hoary; n. a white man; albumen o
an egg; v.t. to whitewash.
whitebait (hwīt'bāt), n. a small
delicate fish.
white book (hwīt book), n. a collection of state-papers, so-called from
the color of the covers, issued by
a government, as England or Ger-
many. Those containing the diplomatic correspondence by these two
countries relating to the outbreak of
the European War in 1914 are especially notable.
whitecap (hwīt'kap), n. a foam-crested
wave; one of a self-constituted tri-
bunal of persons who visit the houses
of offenders against morality and
punish them; one of various birds

ni-ma me- a tu

Artist: Lynne Perrella

White

Artist: Judi Riesch

Lynne's snowy White journal arrived in a frothy flourish, speaking of creamy white dresses and cool satin sashes. I loved the idea of "Women in White" as a theme for my entry, so I began by finding my wedding photo. Taking the lead from Lynne's inside covers, I used photo transfers on fabric and paper, stitching and gluing them together in a sort of loose quilt featuring women and girls in commemorative dresses. Vintage fabrics, in shades of cream to pearl, buttons and old patterns added dimension to the pages. I even used parts of ivory invitations to weddings, graduations and Communions. Tucked inside an ivory vellum envelope in a wisp of lace is a miniature book of white dresses. The young girl in the Communion photo is my mother. Truly a celebration of white as well as life passages.

—Judi Riesch

Artist: Linn C. Jacobs

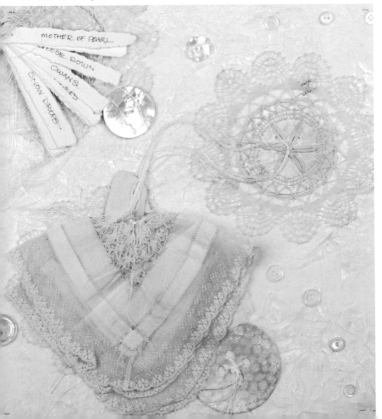

White! Would you have thought to choose white if you were going to take part in a journal collaboration on color? I wouldn't, and doing so gave us a peek into the amazing mind of Lynne Perrella. I started with the crispy paper that I cut into snowflakes and glazed. As I got close to being finished, how I wished that I had worked on a separate piece of paper—it would have been easier to attach everything, then glue the entire page in the journal. I added tags, lovely buttons and the precious antique handkerchief. Recipes from a sweet old 1928 Royal Baking Powder cookbook were tucked inside the hanky.

—Linn C. Jacobs

My local board of education had die-cut machines, where I went to cut out the word "White." When I arrived, a radio at the center was playing full blast and everyone was upset: Planes had crashed into the Pentagon and the World Trade Center. No one knew what had happened to the people on the planes or what would happen next. I met a friend for lunch and we watched the events unfold on the television at the restaurant. Another television played while I attended my Adobe Photoshop class. We watched the buildings collapse and heard about the loss of 200 firemen. By the time I returned to the quiet of my studio, I had reached emotional overload. I worked in silence on this book, thinking of my mother's quiet death at 89 (the figure on the page) and how it affected me. I thought of the many, many violent, early deaths in New York and Washington. I felt the anxiety and unease of not knowing what would happen next. This is what I remember about the work I did on the White journal.

—Anne Bagby

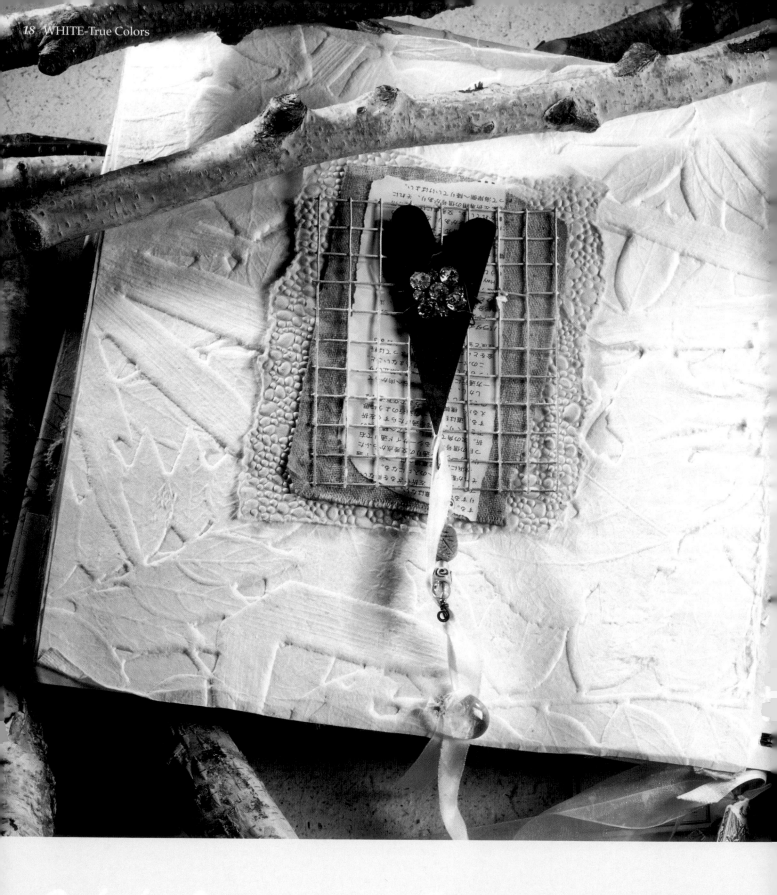

White

I was intrigued by the notion that within the range of white there were infinite tone and textural possibilities. I loved the image of the woman with the dove on each shoulder, and I have two white doves in my studio. This was the starting point for a layout that said "serene and grounded." This is the way that I see my friend, Lynne Perrella, the book's creator. The pages were large and gave

The woman of Tao
Holds oneness in her heart
And her world is at peace
Does not try to please
And therefore shines,
Does not seek attention
And therefore excels,
Does not justify herself
And is therefore trusted,
Does not imitate others
And is therefore herself,
Does not compete
And therefore
No one in the world
Can surpass her.
TAO, 22

me the opportunity to create a "frame" for the photo transferred image. I used muslin a number of times to convey a soft and gentle voice. I felt that a tiny piece of lace would echo the feminine image, so just a hint peeks out from under the frame. The lashed twig is wrapped with shells, ribbon, muslin, and a white feather, and has a touch of silver and rusted wire for contrast. The poem is moving and powerful; it's important for all women and speaks to women artists in particular. The opposite page features a crystal pin that belonged to my grandmother. I felt that the beads, crystal and turquoise contrasted well with the rusted heart. Every detail of this layout has significance for me.

—Lisa Hoffman

Artist: Lisa Renner

Lynne's White journal was the first one I received as we began our adventure. Lynne had done a couple of pages in it, but when I looked at the remaining blank, white pages, knowing I had to use white as my color, I was intimidated. I immediately applied texture using a thin coat of spackle compound. To this, I rubbed burnt sienna acrylic paint around the edges to bring in the eye. Since white signifies the unifying force behind all the colors, I wanted to depict white as the queen, full of innocence and strength. I drew what I imagined her face to look like, coating the surface with a crackle finish. The poem is my definition of white as I see it.

—Lisa Renner

The White journal, my hands-down favorite of the bunch, was a joy to work in. I loved what the other artists had done before me. For my entry, I couldn't get the lyrics from Billy Idol's "White Wedding" out of my head so I decided to go with it. I transferred images of Billy and a woman's face and an old church to fabric. I collaged the woman, a funky wedding dress and veil, and made tulle curtains surrounding the church. I then added lots of bridal leaves and laces that I had left over from making wedding dresses, and a sheer ribbon that contained the song lyrics.

—Keely Barham

Artist: Keely Barham

White

Lynne's White journal was astounding! Who would have thought
there could be so much one could do with the color white? I was
excited to try my hand at it as well. Using an image of a Roman
statue as my focal point, I glued vintage buttons in a halo shape,
then painted with white around the halo. As a final touch, I
outlined a little with pencil. I loved the way the buttons were all
white, but different shades of white—pearl, almond, etc.—each
aged with time. Some buttons still even had the threads left in
them from when they once were on a coat or a dress.

—Claudine Hellmuth

I must say that I was the least excited about getting Lynne's White journal before I saw it, but little did I know the inspiration it held. When it arrived, I was flabbergasted by all of the shades of white people used. The White journal seemed to be a magical place you could go to by simply opening the pages. It probably didn't hurt that I was one of the last people to work on it, so I had the added benefit of seeing everyone's pages. I had a lot of fun playing with colors in the framework of white. I obviously took liberties with the color and was very influenced by outsider artwork, but I gave myself permission to do my own thing. That journal actually inspired the color scheme in my bedroom. I just couldn't get it out of my mind.

—Teesha Moore

Of all the colors in the project, white made me wonder the most if I could do my pages. I generally use a good deal of color in everything I do. Once I had the journal in hand, however, it was a piece of (white wedding) cake. I love the square format and the large size, 12"x12". I was also happy with my juxtapositions of beach and snow—both things I find beautiful and ever so soothing. Lastly, the little girl looks like me, ages ago.

—Sarah Fishburn

shells could it be you that i see

Do I see you coming home
coming home to me
Could it be you that I see
coming home to me
From your day by the sea

Do I see your pockets full
pockets full of shells
Could it be you that I see
pockets full of shells
From your day by the sea

do i see your pockets full pockets full of

pockets full of shells from your day by the

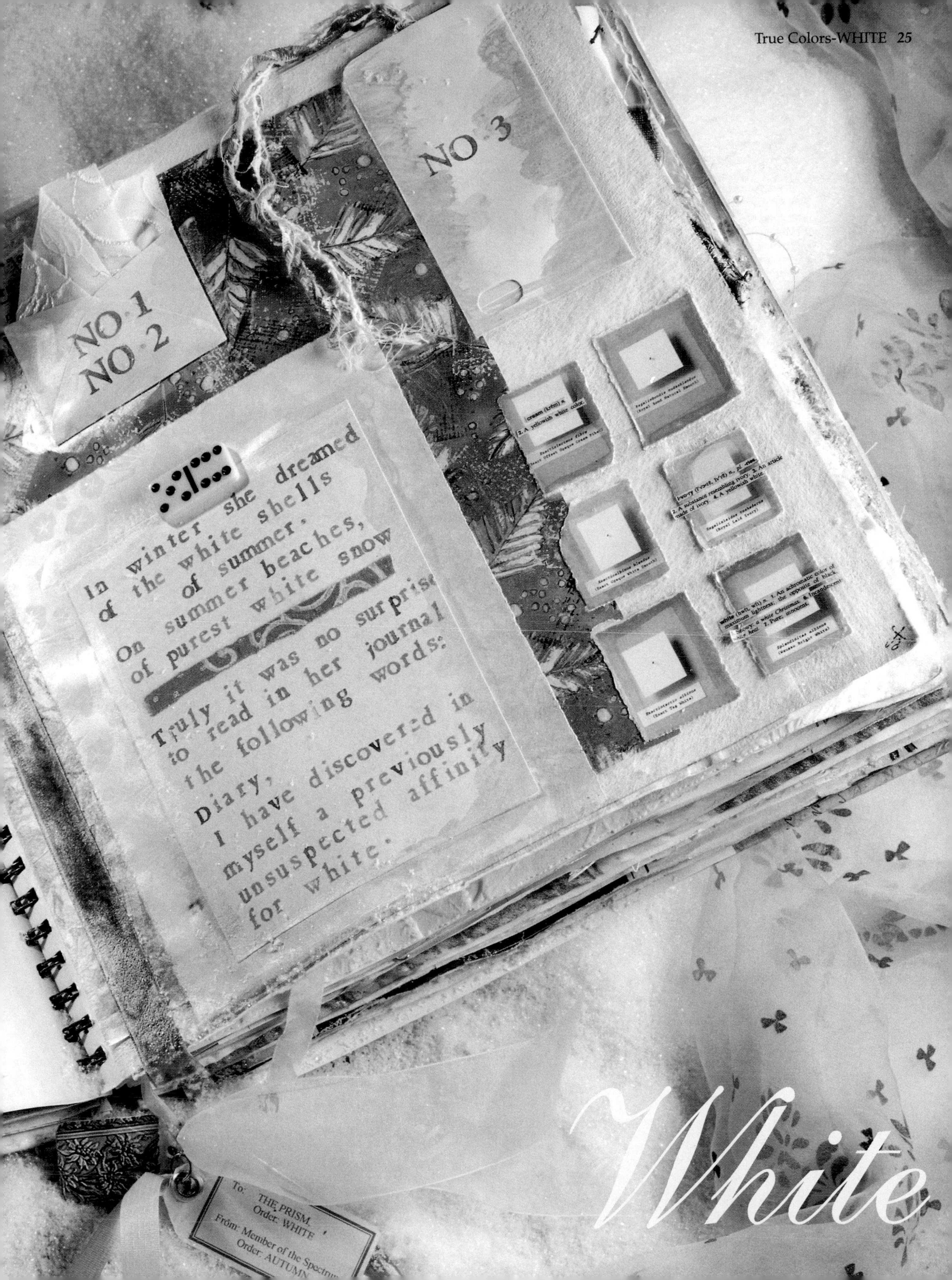

NO. 1
NO. 2

NO. 3

In winter she dreamed
of the white shells
of summer,
On summer beaches,
of purest white snow

Truly it was no surprise
to read in her journal
Diary,
I have discovered in
myself a previously
unsuspected affinity
for white.

White

To: THE PRISM.
Order: WHITE
From: Member of the Spectrum
Order: AUTUMN

Artist: Monica Riffe

While the White journal was in my hands, I saw the world through a white filter, noticing the variety and textures of white: antique lace, frosted glass, vellum paper, gesso on canvas, stucco. My obsessive focus, however, didn't make it any easier to start working in this book. I was stuck—until I took Lynne's book up to my cabin in the Rocky Mountains. Now, this is not a cabin with indoor plumbing: It has an outhouse, and the outhouse walls are decorated with photographs that, over time and exposure to the elements, have faded, some of them almost completely into white. A few of the more weathered photos caught my eye, particularly a vision of swans disappearing into a mist. This image became the catalyst I needed to start my pages in the White journal. As I glued selected papers down, an excerpt from a Simon and Garfunkel song came to mind: "I have a photograph. Preserve your memories; they're all that's left you." This seemed like an apt quote for an entry in Lynne's journal, because she lost her mother to Alzheimer's—a disease that robs people of their memories.

—Monica Riffe

Artist: Lynne Perrella

Artist: Nina Bagley

Oh. White! Pristine, simple. Not. At least, not at first. I swabbed a light, watered-down acrylic wash of white over the blank background to lighten things up a bit, then pulled out assorted cream and white imagery from my stockpile. What struck me most was a Victorian photo album page. I inserted an image I had transferred to watercolor paper of a geisha girl, whose face was porcelain white, and whose cap bore trailing tendrils of the whitest ribbon-like braids. I attached the album page with mother-of-pearl buttons. Using large vintage grocery store produce stamps over the white page background I stamped in white over white, the lettering is bold yet subtle. Thank you, Lynne, for nudging us beyond our own safe limits.

—*Nina Bagley*

The White journal came so beautifully wrapped; it even interested my cat, who sat beside me as I savored each page created by those who worked before me on this gem. This book was quite a challenge for me. I'm quite generous with color in my own work, so working with a white palette was a stretch. I explored white from its creams to its brilliance. With feelings of September 11th still fresh in my heart, I evoked the dove as a prayer for peace, and the symbol of the skull to bring about the circle of rebirth through death.

—*Karen Michel*

Artist: Karen Michel

A red-haired artist, Sarah Fishburn, created the spiral-bound Red journal with a collage of a flower child printed on the cover.

Red ignited all kinds of ideas in the artists. Red reminded Lynne Perrella of her mother's favorite lipstick; it inspired Monica Riffe to create a page in the happy, kitschy style of the 1950s, with red plaid oil tablecloths and red rickrack trim. It prompted Judi Riesch to alter a haunting, brooding image of Red Riding Hood, who looks just a little bit demonic in her red cape.

Somber and seductive, retro and romantic, passionate and patriotic, red is a riot of differing emotions.

Karen Michel called this journal "a wandering sort of valentine." Indeed, each artist's entry is a work of love.

No matter what passions this color may arouse, one thing's for certain: One cannot stay neutral on the subject of red.

Firecrackers in July.
The color of royalty,
the color of blood.
Love *and* the devil.
Ripe and delicious Red.

Red

ORIGINATING ARTIST:
Sarah Fishburn

In its myriad brilliant shades, and its more subtle ones, too, red represents a passion for life and fun. Red makes the world a jazzier place!

For the cover of the Red journal, I wanted to convey the pure beauty of the color. At the same time, I played with the idea of a child who might choose to color everything in her coloring book a single color—red! I love the part of making or altering a book where I get to give it a title, and with this journal it came to me in a second—"My Coloring Book: Red." Woo-hoo! Printed onto a transparency, my cover art is both attached and embellished with some fabulously fun vintage buttons, including one of hand-painted porcelain and a few yellow and red bakelite beauties.

I incorporate the color red in nearly every piece I make, though sometimes it's no more than a hint in the hand-tinted lips of a little girl in an old photo, or a soft border of rose-colored ink framing a page.

This was not my first collaborative book experience; I've done more than a few since and intend to continue working in group projects. I never felt stuck on any of the *True Colors* books. I always had an immediate idea for what I wanted to say or do. I didn't pay much attention to the style of the owner. Rather, I stayed true to my own style. In the few instances where I didn't stay true to myself, I felt the work was weaker.

A good collaboration is one where you wake up early because you can't wait to get started on your next section, or stay up all night to finish that last little bit. And you can't wait to share what you've done with your fellow collaborators. You wait ever so eagerly to hear them say, "Yay! My book came today and I can't believe how gorgeous—or amazing—or fun it is, and exactly HOW did you do, well, whatever it was you did!" And when you get your own book back, you can't stop stealing time away from new projects to look at it. "OK, if I just finish this" —whatever IT is—"I can look at my book for, ohhh, say 15 minutes!" You show it to anyone who displays even the tiniest bit of curiosity; you find occasions to bring up the subject in general conversation. You find yourself collaborating with others.

It does get a bit tricky when 15 artists are involved in a project. The logistics can be unwieldy, yet the results are priceless. It really helps to keep one's sense of perspective and humor close at hand.

Personally, I like my collaborations with a dash of irony, a splash of cologne, a twist of fate and a nice hot Swamp Rocket (a drink I made up using Tang and Midori that's become amazingly popular around these parts and elsewhere).

— Sarah Fishburn

i'd rather have
[red] roses on my
table than diamonds
on my neck.

emma goldman

this book was begun
in May of the year
two thousand and one
by sarah fishburn

The Girls' Companion

big

STOP

cherries lips
and silken slips

color RED

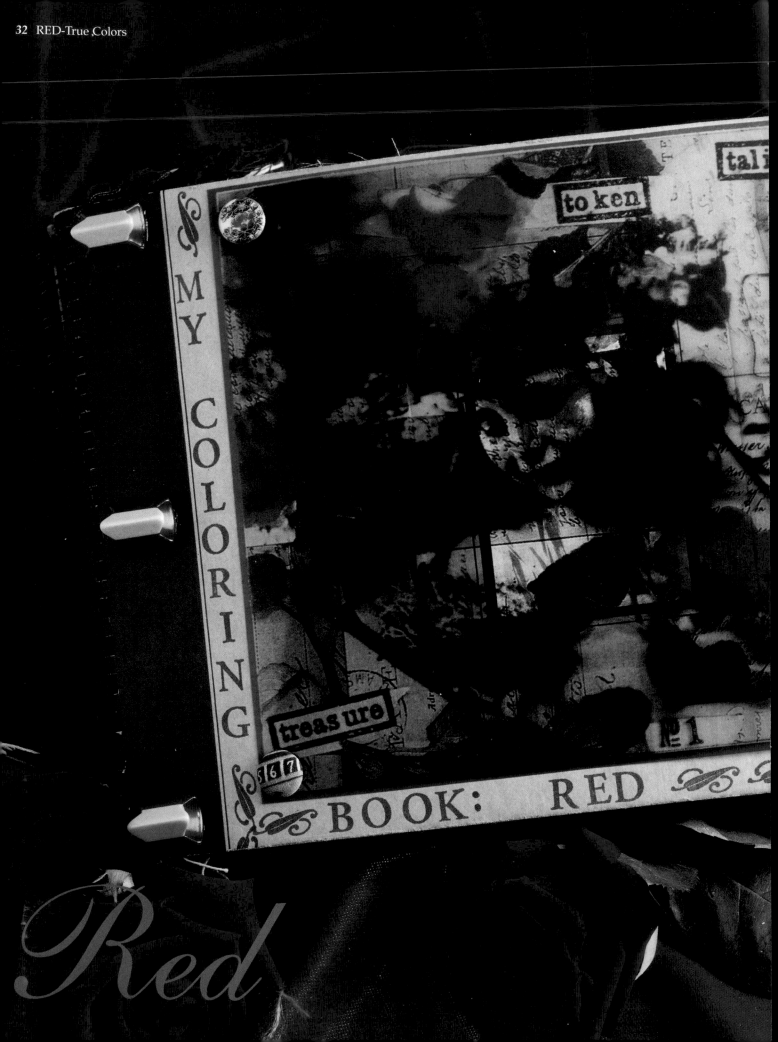

MY COLORING BOOK: RED

to ken

tal

treasure

Red

in pretty colours

THE·AUTHOR'S·BOX
·(THIS·IS·TOO·LARGE

COVER
SLIDES

Artist: Sarah Fishburn

POSTALE
E - POST CARD

Artist: Claudine Hellmuth

Evoking passion and the heart, this book conjured a wandering sort of valentine. It's a well-traveled valentine that carries the pictures of its adventure with its heart.

—Karen Michel

At the time I worked on the Red journal, I was doing a lot of valentine card designs for a publishing company, so I had pinks, reds, and valentines on my mind. I was also experimenting with unstretched canvas. I decided to create my piece for Sarah on unstretched canvas, and I really liked its raw edges—it looked so "found" to me.

—Claudine Hellmuth

HANDLE WITH CARE

सावधान

Artist: Karen Michel

Artist: Karen Michel

Artist: Teesha Moore

Artist: Marylinn Kelly

I had been anxiously awaiting the Red journal from the get-go because red velvet is a huge turn-on for me. I was envisioning this Moulin Rouge feeling in anticipation of receiving the journal. At the time it arrived, I had decided to start doing my own kind of art in each journal, so I just played in the Red journal like it was my own. Because the pages were black, I used my favorite journaling paper (Fabriano Uno paper from Hot Press). I was able to journal on the paper and glue it into the book. Using paper I was familiar with freed me up. I was also able to sew on the pages because they were separate. Again, fabric crept into the artwork because of the richness of the colors.

—Teesha Moore

I had just seen the movie Moulin Rouge when the Red journal arrived. It was rich with color and stories and had grown thick with attached objects. I took all of that as encouragement to try and interpret the movie—its color, movement and texture—in paper. Over a background of paint layers and painted lace, I fashioned cancan skirts out of gathered strips of paper. Approaching the project in this way was a strong connection to paper crafts I had done as a girl, a combination of paper dolls and costuming. I tried for the excess and energy on the page that I felt were a huge part of the movie's appeal.

—Marylinn Kelly

Red

Ahhh, Red. I had seen Lynne Perrella's Past Lives line of rubber stamps and couldn't wait to use her "Maiden Voyage" image. Somehow, the haunting and poetic image of a woman's profile just said "red," so I waited to receive Sarah's book and jumped in. I needed a color with depth and mystery; the red had to have a deep, burgundy-maroon cast. I wanted to support the story of a woman waiting, yet remove any hint of impatience or anxiety. We see her gazing out over a scene of ships at sea, which I scanned from a clip-art book. The main images on each page were scanned onto transparent acetate. The next move involved texture, and what better choice than real seashells, collected from the East Coast? I added twigs and sticks painted in the same color that appears on the background, and a broken glob of sealing wax. I loved the fact that the wax had cracked, giving it an authentic and old appearance. The old quote flew into my head the moment I saw the image of ships at sea. How lucky that the quote included the word red.

—Lisa Hoffman

Artist: Lisa Hoffman

RED SKY
AT NIGHT---

SAILORS
DELIGHT

My mother loved the color red. Her favorite lipstick shade was "Hot Tomato." She preferred red nail polish, and had a favorite red "Christmas slip" that she would wear with her holiday dress-up clothes. There was often a photo of Marion pulling her hem up just a bit, showing that saucy little hem of red lace. As soon as Sarah's journal arrived, I knew I wanted to create an entry about my mother. I was instantly taken by the amount of "danglies" emerging from the Red journal. Ribbons, fibers and strands of all descriptions led me to fine-tune my idea, telling a story about my mother when she lived in New Mexico as a young woman. The deep fringe of her vintage red woolen serape gave me the idea to photocopy the actual fabric on a copy machine, and then add touchable strands of threads, cascading over a well-loved photo of mom. I went into her old scrapbooks and borrowed a photo of her, standing amongst cactus and cottonwoods, wearing a sombrero and a flirty grin. The two envelopes, on either side of the photo, contain stories and remembrances and the tender lyrics from the song "Red River Valley." I wanted to add something that would document my own memorable time in New Mexico, so I pulled out a group of milagros that I found in Taos and glued them in place. "From this valley they say you are going ... I will miss your bright eyes and sweet smile."

—Lynne Perrella

Artist: Lynne Perrella

Sarah's journal was my first assignment. When her book arrived, I announced to the group: "Oh, fortunate me! Sarah's work of wonder has arrived. It's a magnificent array of richness ... color, texture and sentiment in warm cozy reds. It's already whispering an invitation to play that doesn't even scare me. I have to admit that red seems out of my realm. Time to crawl out of my box and break open the paints I gathered especially for Sarah's book." It was truly a gift to be faced with black journal pages, a sign of welcome. My first spread began with a collection of Madonna cuttings from a Botticelli book. Their deep dark reds were asking to be in Sarah's book. I needed a song to accompany the pages, so I went with "Let It Be," and included the lyrics as well as a recording. I enjoyed playing with metallic paints on the black paper.

—Michelle Ward

Artist: Michelle Ward

I know I have the body of a weak and feeble woman, but I have the heart and stomach of a King.

Red

Artist: Anne Bagby

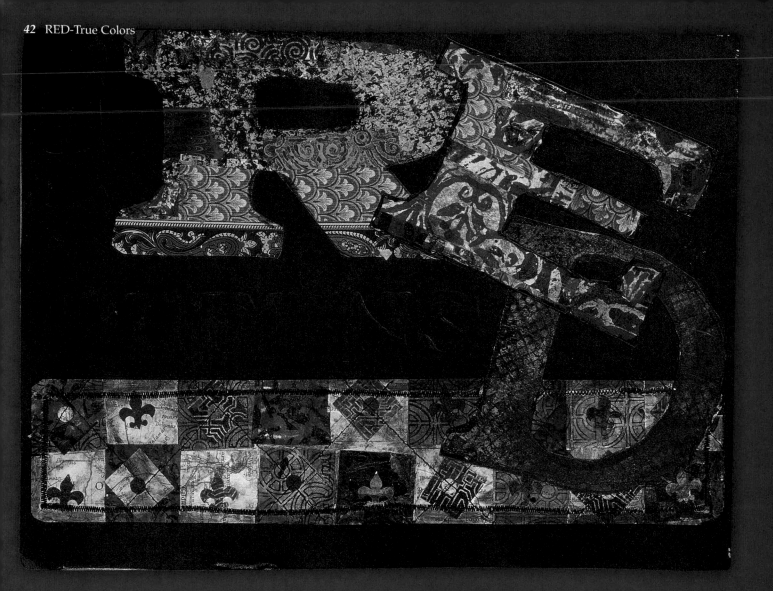

Artist: Anne Bagby

This is a great color for a book. All that excitement and emotion. I was full of ideas and ambition and couldn't seem to stop. This was definitely my "too much is not enough" page. Just the idea of red seemed to give me permission to include everything! My theme was the red queen, and I put down anything that came to mind. Much of my time on this project was spent quilting the paper, but I didn't think the stitching results were worth the effort. I think this was the only project where I used a traditional image and transferred it, rather than doing the drawing myself. The drawing of Queen Elizabeth was too perfect to alter, but I ended up doing an extra page with my own drawing of Queen Elizabeth.

—Anne Bagby

I had plans for Sarah's Red journal long before it arrived. I knew Sarah loves images of young girls with red hair (just like her) and Little Red Riding Hood has always been a favorite of mine. I still have a vivid memory of myself at 6 years old on Halloween, walking back to school after lunch in my scarlet red cape and dress with a crisp white apron, holding a basket of cookies. This fairytale intrigued and frightened me at the same time—similar to the feelings I had about playing with the color red! So imagine my excitement when I discovered a wonderful sepia photograph of Red Riding Hood taken by Lewis Carroll in 1857, in a book called Reflections in a Looking Glass: A Centennial Celebration of Lewis Carroll, Photographer *(Aperture). This photo just had to be shared, so I altered it with paints, pastels, feathers, and stamped images of leaves and ferns to create a deep, forest-like feel to the pages.*

—Judi Riesch

Red

Artist: Judi Riesch

Little Red Riding Hood photo:
©Harry Ransom Humanities Research Center

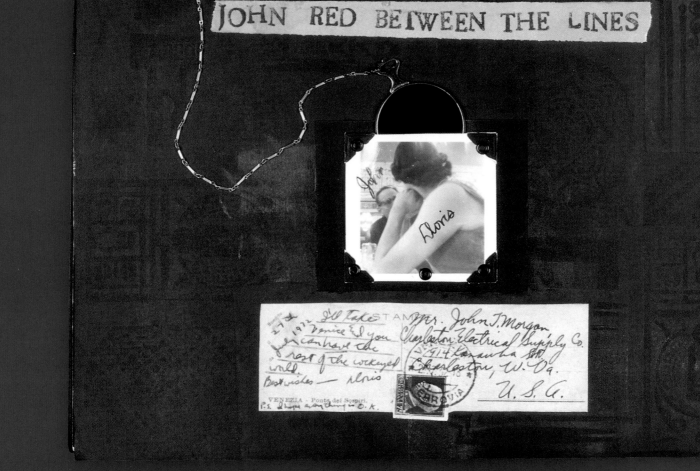

The "story" for my first page in the Red journal stemmed from a single little vintage photograph I unearthed in a photo album that I'd found on eBay. A woman's back is turned to the camera; she is engaged in conversation with a man whose face is only partially seen from behind her forearm. I gave her the name of Doris and called him John, based on a separate slim little postcard I've treasured from Venice that reads, "I'll take Venice and you can have the rest of the cockeyed world. Best wishes, Doris." It was addressed to John, with a "P.S. I hope everything is okay" tacked on in tiny writing at the bottom. Well, I wonder how John felt about that? So I stamped out in bold letters, "John red (sic) between the lines." I felt for him, I truly did.

My second page was simply a vintage book cover of some young girls in a motor car with a background of red. Knowing Sarah's love of old books, I let the beauty of the cover speak for itself and slipped it into a vellum envelope that I had attached with red eyelets to a red-ink stamped page. Red on black. Lovely.

The third page, "a red letter day," was simple as well—an envelope attached with ribbon to a red-stamped background, with a very old photograph bordered with red lace imagery of my own stamp design. Using another of my designs that I'd stamped with permanent ink on transparency film that reads "place photo here," I cut the design out and attached pink eyelets over a little girl's dress that I had colored pink. A lesson again in branching out!

—Nina Bagley

Teesha Moore picked two of the loudest, brightest hues on the color wheel for her playful journal. "I wanted this to be an explosion of color!" she writes. To get the party started, she covered her journal in eye-popping pink and orange fabric, stitching pockets on the front for holding game pieces and small toys.

When the artists saw her outrageous journal, they knew it was playtime. Lisa Hoffman got into the spirit of the journal, decorating her pages with a mix of kitschy objects, including loteria cards, a Mexican chocolate box, soap wrappers, and black lace. She writes, "… before I knew it, I was listening to salsa music and slamming down the layers as though I was possessed by the spirit of Carmen Miranda."

Lynne got silly and adorned her entry with an empty pink and orange doughnut box, complete with photocopies of actual doughnuts festooned with the appropriate-colored sprinkles. Judi Riesch created a page inspired by pink bubble gum, while Anne Bagby played with paper dolls. The Hot Pink & Orange journal was the place to cut loose and cut up, to have fun and let the art happen without trying too hard—just as Teesha wanted it.

Hot Pink
& Orange

It's a 1960s flashback.
A journey to India.
It crackles like a high-voltage wire.
Neon pink and electric orange
combine into one trippy book.
Time to party.

ORIGINATING ARTIST:
Teesha Moore

When I was trying to pick a color, I couldn't settle on just one. For me, color is all about having at least two contrasting hues bouncing off each other. That's exhilarating! I chose pink and orange because that color combination has always excited me. When I see the two colors together, my heart races. I've always been drawn to Eastern Indian-inspired artwork—the people, the dance, the food, the music and, of course, the colors. I think I must have lived in India in another life.

At the time *True Colors* began, I was making journals out of fabric. Pink and orange seemed like the perfect choice because I have collected a huge assortment of fabrics in those colors. I added the pockets for the book's journey, thinking the other artists might like to tuck in odds and ends. I just used whatever was in front of me on my desk without a whole lot of thought. I never put much thought into my work. It seems to work better when I step aside and let the creativity happen. Because my studio is pink and orange, the thought crossed my mind that this journal would make a nice addition to the décor once it was complete.
***
I wanted to exude a party feeling with my journal, so I started it out with a poem. I also wanted people to leave no white borders, because plain white borders bug me. I wanted this to be an explosion of color! I used a combination of collage, watercolors, acrylics and crayons, as usual.
***
When Lynne Perrella asked if I might be interested in a color journal collaboration, I jumped at the chance. The idea that we would each have our own space to create

without someone else covering up or altering our work was appealing to me, and the notion of having to stick with certain colors seemed like a welcome challenge. I suppose the part I liked the least about the project was all the e-mails. While I truly appreciate all the girls involved and their stories, I always seemed to have too much else on my plate to even read half of them. I was in it for the art more than the friendship. Sometimes I wish I could slow down long enough to smell the roses and relish the friendships, but that remains an area for me to work on.

For me, the biggest challenge of working on each journal was feeling that I needed to create in the style of the artist who started the journal. For that reason, I was always frozen when trying to create pages. I didn't feel I could do my own thing. The deadline would come, and I would have to whip something up in a hurry. About halfway through the project, I expressed my despair to the group, and someone said something (I wish I could remember what …) which made me realize that what each artist wanted in her journal was my artwork, not my attempt at her own style of artwork. From that point on, it was a piece of cake and became a much more fun project.

To me, these journals seemed more like artist books. The pages in my own personal journals are always finished off with lots of words and writing in all the spare spots on the page. I felt that all the pages I did for this project lacked that personal element. I would have written my jibber jabber on the pages, but I felt they wanted more of an "art" book. Thus, I felt most of the pages I did were unfinished.

—Teesha Moore

Artist: Teesha Moore

Artist: Karen Michel

Hot Pink & Orange

I've always been drawn to Teesha's art and use of imagery, so I felt right at home with this journal. What's more electric than this color combination? This journal had a great fabric cover equipped with little pockets holding toys, which really inspired me to get in and play with the colors. I added a hot pink paper hat I had saved from Christmas and created a playground for a very unlikely angel. It's all about the jive.

—Karen Michel

This layout was supposed to be deeply mysterious and romantic, but the "Wild Street Carnival" side of me kept leaping out onto the studio table. My first page included a Pablo Neruda quote, real flowers and a vintage photo of the sea. This was as tame as it got. I think that the black lace trim did it—before I knew it, I was listening to salsa music and slamming down the layers as though I was possessed by the spirit of Carmen Miranda! There is a bright pink soap wrapper from the Hotel Caleta, where I stayed in the '70s, a Mexican chocolate box, a loteria card or two, more black lace (this time wider and bolder) and these HUGE, trashy silk flowers, for just the right mood.

—Lisa Hoffman

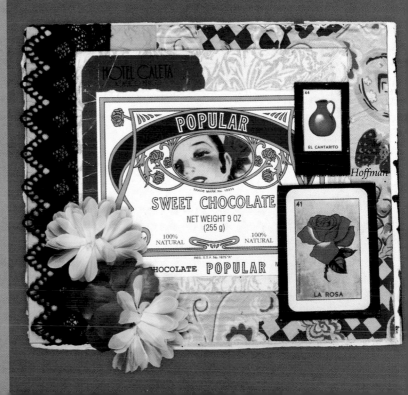

Hot Pink & Orange

Although I was not scheduled to receive Teesha's journal first, I got a "sneak peek" of it while visiting Lynne the month we began the collaboration. It was a wonderful cloth-covered book in funky shades of hot pink and orange that made my blood race. How would I ever work in these colors? A trip to a paper store in New York City yielded some interesting selections, and I returned to Atlanta a bit calmer, ready to face this journal when it came my way. When I received it, one thing came to mind: bubble gum! Using fabric for the background, I altered a copy of an endearing photo of a girl with striped socks that reminded me of Teesha's hand-drawn characters, and the bubble gum spread was under way. I created a small book with neon covers to write the text from an old jump rope rhyme: "Bubble gum, bubble gum in a dish. How many pieces do you wish?" The pastels I used over the paint even gave a "dusty" finish to the pages, just like it feels to unwrap that little square of Double Bubble Gum.

—Judi Riesch

Artist: Monica Riffe

Artist: Keely Barham

If there were a yearbook of **True Colors** artists, Teesha would get my vote for "Most Playful." In her whimsical style, she invited us to have fun, to go out of bounds in our use of color, and to let our art literally spill off the pages of her book. I had a blast playing at her journal "party." And I now notice how often pink and orange appear together. When I saw the movie Monsoon Wedding, I kept thinking, "Teesha would LOVE this movie, it is so pink and orange!"

—Monica Riffe

I came across the perfect orange with pink polka dot fabric at a store and said, "This is so Teesha." It became the background for my art quilt, which I machine-embroidered with squiggly lines. I then added the masked figures, which were inspired by one of my favorite Rubber Moon stamps. I used velvet leaves that were the perfect colors on the figures. Lastly, I added little pictures that I had drawn and then transferred to fabric. This was one of my favorite pieces.

—Keely Barham

Hot Pink & Orange

Artist: Sarah Fishburn

original

Artist: Sarah Fishburn

I really liked my concept for these pages. They are based on a quote I paraphrased from fashion designer Diana Vreeland, "Pink & Orange are the Navy Blue of India." I was attempting a brilliantly garish illustration of that quote. I feel my colors were successful, but the pages lack cohesion. They are jarring and discordant to me. I would like to do another piece eventually, recycling the same concept, and see if I can make it work.

—Sarah Fishburn

I received the Hot Pink & Orange journal two weeks after the serenity of White! My eyes popped, and I immediately got to work. I was inspired because I knew Teesha loves dolls. I used some fabric I had painted for the doll's dress, sewing a little clear pocket on the front to hold a small book. The hands are made from reduced copies of my own hands, attached to fibers representing the doll's arms. The background is acrylic paint in various shades of pink, orange and yellow accented in white using Judi-Kins' chicken wire stamp.

—Lisa Renner

Hot Pink & Orange

Artist: Lisa Renner

I collected numerous pink and orange patches and had a great idea for the book before it even arrived. On my own, I would never do a painting in pink and orange, so I loved working in these colors for this project! The book didn't disappoint; it fairly danced around the studio, so VERY pink and orange. However, I couldn't get my ideas to gel completely. My page looks too staid for a Teesha book. I wanted paper dolls that were playful, but they turned out to have a serious look. I decided the dolls represented muses, suggesting what is needed for success in our artistic endeavors: effort, joy, risk and skill. In fact, I think Teesha embodies these very qualities.

—Anne Bagby

Hot Pink & Orange

Artist: Lynne Perrella

Artist: Marylinn Kelly

Teesha's journal was the first one I received. The excitement of opening the carton and finding her riotous, joyous, playful journal was doubled by the fact that Judi happened to be visiting me at the time. That afternoon, we went to the doughnut shop to start collecting all the "art supplies" I would need to create my doughnut-themed pages. We were given a whole armload of free doughnut boxes, and I think we caused quite a stir as we stood there, discussing which doughnuts were the right color for the project (apparently, most people do not purchase doughnuts by color). Later, I arrived at my copy center with the chosen doughnuts in a Styrofoam cooler and a spray bottle of Windex. The copy center folks are used to my high jinx, but I think the doughnut project broke new ground. I made plenty of prints of the various doughnuts and had great fun going through my stash of beads and sequins, trying to find the appropriate sprinkles. The palette of hot pink and orange also reminded me of a paper dress I had in the sixties, so that story was illuminated in a little pullout accordion book housed in a small mesh handbag and glued to the page. Touchable elements, interactive pull-downs and moveable parts are a wonderful way to engage the viewer, and were my way of continuing the feeling of delight and play in Teesha's journal.
—Lynne Perrella

COLOR=Memory
(Reprinted from Lynne's entry)

I started thinking about hot pink and orange, and soon I was reminded of a paper dress that I bought back in 1966. It was the Andy Warhol influence, I'm sure. It was a white sleeveless "tent" dress with huge hot pink and orange polka dots. WHAT was I thinking? Anyhow, I thought it was just the coolest; certainly, the closest I was going to come to buying a Warhol original. I couldn't wait to have an excuse to wear the dress …

I knew a roguish young man named Phil Brown. Phil was not my actual boyfriend—but he made my pulse race, and could reduce me to a warm quivering mass by just flashing his devilish grin. As we talked on the phone, setting up a date, I told him that I planned to wear the paper dress that evening. When he came to the door to pick me up, he pulled a tiny pair of snob-nose children's scissors from his pocket, and made a little "snip snip" motion with his hands, mid-air. I thought he was delicious, and maybe even a little dangerous. Why, goodness: This young man was planning to turn my new dress into confetti! Instead, we had a glorious date, and all was well. Years later, I noticed that I would think of Phil every time I passed a Dunkin' Donuts store. The jolly hot pink and orange rounded logo seemed to suggest the long-ago polka dots—and a simpler time when a girl could buy a paper dress for a couple of bucks, and feel kicky and flirtatious and full of confetti.

Phillip Draper Brown: Where Are You NOW?

Teesha's journal brought up a strong childhood memory that I translated into paper. One Christmas, my artist mother announced that we were having a Mexican Christmas. The familiar pipe cleaner candy canes and shiny glass balls were replaced on the tree by painted tin ornaments and bright papier-mâché acrobat dolls, their hot pink costumes and orange hair accented with lots of glitter. Though we eventually went back to our old decorations, the acrobats stayed, having become friends. Since the word "play" is a mainstay of Teesha's vocabulary, I wanted to have fun. I made a jointed, paper version of an acrobat doll, attached over a background of orange and pink paper strips and a transparency of three of the dolls. Drawn and cut-out flowers, glitter and a quote about the body being "a fiesta" told my Pink & Orange story.
—Marylinn Kelly

Long shadows at twilight. A bicyclist stops to admire the fading colors. Many of the artists' entries in the Sunset journal reflect their awareness of the transitory beauty of sunsets.

Marylinn Kelly chose Sunset for her theme, opening the door to a riot of brilliant colors. She painted the cover of her spiral-bound journal "the color of night just before dark," adding a twilight sky painted on muslin, then sent the book on its way.

Sunset allowed the artists to play with vivid shades of gold, orange, red, turquoise, and blue. "Intense hues," Lynne Perrella calls them. Sensing that this was their chance to cut loose with color, many did just that: Teesha created a big, glorious orange sun with spiky red rays. "I could use any variety of colors I wanted, something I found myself crying out to do on all of the journals," she writes. "I don't like to be limited." Michelle Ward's entry, with its stamped images of sun gods, is pure gold. For Lynn and the journal's creator, Marylinn, sunsets evoked memories of youthful romantic encounters, when passions were new and, well, intense. They recalled their first heady taste of romance and their mysterious passage into adulthood.

The Sunset journal captures those fleeting moments when something is ending, but another, magical thing is about to begin.

Sunset

A final burst of light and color.
A diminishing glow
on the horizon.
Encroaching darkness.
Sunset signifies both a beginning
and an end. Carpe diem.

ORIGINATING ARTIST:
Marylinn Kelly

Sunset reminds me of the summer I was 18. In my mind, I see an August sky. I'm riding in a sports car, going to the Hollywood Bowl. Just before the sun disappears on this summer night, the air becomes soft, the rough edges of heat and smog transform into a gentle moment that you can feel on your skin. Summers still have these moments. That particular summer was a time of dizzying possibility, romance, and a walk across the bridge from child to grownup. The word sunset holds all the color, all the music, all the promise of that one season. "The light and shadow mystery of a summer-color night," I stamped on my journal's first page. Nearly 40 years later, I still feel its magic. Sunset has stories to tell.

***

I had no fabric in the colors I wanted for the cover of my Sunset journal, so I painted muslin with acrylics, creating the strata of that summer night. My sunset will always have the silhouettes of palm trees and dots of stars. I can't say what inspired the cover's form; I know I wanted it to be a fabric postcard. The painted blue of the journal cover is the color of night just before dark. The polka dots are reminders of the playfulness, the fun. The only inside page I completed seemed to be evidence of sunset, little bags with intense sunset colors and a sun illustration where all colors meet. Confetti on a cupcake, that's my sunset.

***

This was my first involvement in an art exchange. For part of the time I was not at all sure what was expected of me, and I put a lot of energy into trying to make this an intellectual puzzle with an intellectual answer. I would love to say that every piece I contributed was the perfect rendering of my vision for that journal. But what I do know about my own process is that a thing, whether a story or a drawing or a collage, becomes what it is, not what I think it should be, and no amount of effort or will on my part can change it. Let me add that there was absolutely no external pushing or prodding of any kind. All of this was purely internal. I felt free to do whatever came to me—a great gift. Even the edge of the page wasn't a boundary.

As I watched some of the pieces flow and some move less sure-footedly, I spent a lot of mental time trying to conquer the process rather than embrace it. Learning to be contentedly imperfect is a lesson that comes slowly. I had a strong desire to dazzle and that urge sometimes got in the way of the other desire, to be authentic. After much wrestling, I realized that authenticity would bring me peace, but the effort to dazzle (dazzle whom?) would never be enough. I thought frequently of the expression, "Comparisons are odious." It is not idle talk, for when we compare, we undermine ourselves and our originality. We send ourselves a message that, as is, we are insufficient. My greatest challenge in this project was to make peace with me being me.

—Marylinn Kelly

Artist: Keely Barham

Sunset

*A*s I was anticipating the arrival of Marylinn's Sunset journal, I gave a lot of thought to what I was going to do. There was such a wide range of interpretations in the previous entries—no help there to pin down my pages. I decided to draw a sun face that I then transferred to fabric. Once I saw the printed fabric sun, I got the idea to make a removable doll. She had beaded sun ray hair and a fancy dress. This gave me the idea of the "Miss Sunset" theme, so I made her a banner to wear. My favorite part is how the skirt opens up to reveal a dancing moon face man.

—Keely Barham

I had ideas of creating a muted golden sunset in Marylinn's book until it arrived; the journal cover was so bright and fun and colorful I felt like my preconceived notions would have to be reconsidered. As I paged through the contents, I was thrilled to come across the last entry by Sarah. Her offering was soft and rich—a sign I could proceed with my sunset plans. I chose the title song from Chariots of Fire as my musical soundtrack, and played off the Greek tale of the sun being led across the sky by a charioteer for my imagery.

—Michelle Ward

INTO THE **SUNSETS** TURQUOISE MARGE
THE **MOON** DIPS LIKE A PEARL BARGE

INTO THE FIELDS IN **GHOSTGRAY** GOWN

THE YOUNG EYED **DUSK** COMES

SLOWLY DOWN

HER **APRON** FILLED WITH **STARS** SHE STANDS

AND ONE OR TWO SLIP FROM HER HANDS

Artist: Judi Riesch

When Marylinn's Sunset journal appeared, I was totally stumped. I was captivated by the book's whimsical feel and the bright ice cream colors, but it sat for days on my coffee table as I tried to find a creative direction. Quite by accident, I was looking at some old poetry books and came across a piece by Madison Julius Cawein. It was the jump-start I needed. My entry would be soft and simple, just like the final stages of a sunset. I put down the "turquoise marge" with layers of paint and pages from an old Farmer's Almanac. The image of "young-eyed dusk" came from a very old photo of an outdoor theater production. Her ghost-gray gown and open wings provided the ideal hiding place for the mother-of-pearl star buttons. "... Her apron filled with stars she stands. And one or two slip from her hands."

—Judi Riesch

Marylinn was the amazingly wonderful woman who I mailed my journals to when I was done working on them. I talked to her every now and then via e-mail and was always charmed by her insight and kindness. It was a joy to finally receive her Sunset journal late in the game. I fell in love with Keely's "Sun Momma," and it took me more than a few days to get beyond it! I went through my cache of painted and paste papers and used several to get started. I over-painted, stamped and re-touched the papers with acrylics and penned in a couple of sunset quotes. A little softening touch was needed, and—voila—I added the silky threads as colorful rays of a sunset, also a faint echo of Keely's wonderful textile piece!

—Linn C. Jacobs

Artist: Linn C. Jacobs

Artist: Lynne Perrella

Sunset—the most romantic time of the day. The moody streaks of intense hues, the unexpected combinations of colors, all looking so right, and the anticipation of evening and all that it may bring. A couple rest close together. Her gown glitters in the glow of the car radio dial. The lyric surrounds them, "You're my Cone-y Is-land Ba-by." These journal pages were done to describe and define the feeling of long-ago adolescence, and to recall and reclaim the magic of all that. I have gotten to know Marylinn over the past few years by phone and by e-mail, and we have conducted a kindred dialog about the significance and importance of telling our stories. I wanted my pages to not only evoke a real-life setting, but also the feeling of people floating in the clouds; in a sense, becoming part of the sunset. I used Xerox transfers, plus washes of acrylic paints, Prismacolor pencils, and applied iridescent sequins to emphasize the feeling of being lost in the moment, swept away on a warm summer night. "You're my lucky star, that's what you are. ...You're my girl."

—Lynne Perrella

I was very excited by these colors. They inspired me to write a poem about the "Lady of Dusk," who I pictured facing a blank canvas of sky, and "with sweeping hand released, painting a bronzed and purple dusk…" The art was built around the poem. I used joss paper and dropped watercolor inks onto it, then glued it to the pages. Acrylic paints in purple, ochre, gold, and blue were added. I had picked up a postcard of Winged Victory when I was in Paris, so I copied the wings onto a piece of acetate. The poem was copied on top of it. The acetate was then attached with eyelets.

—Lisa Renner

Artist: Lisa Renner

As a counterpoint to the Sunset theme of Marylinn's journal, I depicted the earth setting from the vantage point of the moon. I used sunset colors and incorporated some of my favorite collage materials: strips of dried acrylic paints and aerial maps, which I adhered with gel medium to create a moonscape.

The hardest thing about the **True Colors** project was sending the books on. I typically tried to show them to as many friends as possible. After I finished "Earth-set," I figured out a way to savor my page for a bit longer: I scanned the image, and turned it into a desktop display for my computer monitor.

—Monica Riffe

Sunset

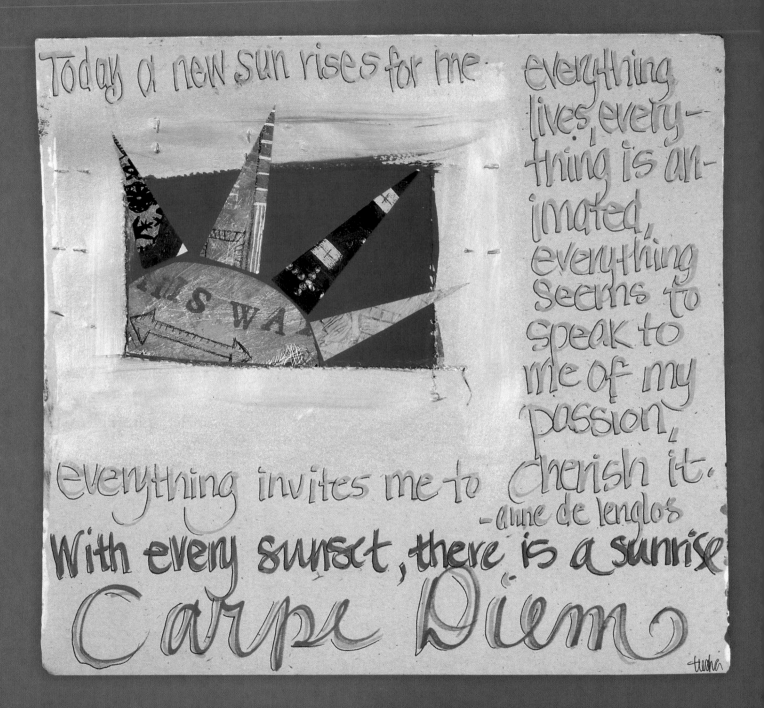

Today a new sun rises for me. everything lives, everything is animated, everything seems to speak to me of my passion, everything invites me to cherish it.
—anne de lenglos

With every sunset, there is a sunrise
Carpe Diem

I decided to try something different in Marylinn's journal. I love to experiment in journals, so I found an old collage I did that seemed to fit the sunset theme and copied it onto a piece of transparency. I did this at Kinko's on a color copier. Then I sewed fabric to the page and attached the transparency over the top. This seemed more interesting than pasting a color copy to the page. It also made the page interactive, a feature I like to add to journals. Sunset was fun because I could use any variety of colors I wanted, something I found myself crying out to do on all of the journals. I don't like to be limited.
—Teesha Moore

Wrapped in fabric and tied with a ribbon, the Yellowgreen & Copper journal was Linn Jacobs' gift to the artists. Linn wanted to give them the freedom to work unencumbered by binding or the fear that they might mess up someone else's pages. Her solution was the unusual portfolio format. In the words of Michelle Ward: "A creative offering of loose paper in a fabric enclosure, tied with ribbons and bells, Linn's journal announced liberty!"

The liberated artists were free to explore an array of mediums and techniques. Twists of lime, copper pumpkins, songbirds in autumn—they found all kinds of ways to interpret the color scheme. Lisa Renner created a small journal-within-a-journal that she tucked in a wire mesh pocket and embellished with beads. Claudine Hellmuth stitched a row of beads to the bottom of her simply beautiful leaf collage. Several artists added coins, bells, buttons, and other melodic charms to the journal.

Let freedom ring.

Yellowgreen

&Copper

The tinkling sound of pennies, buttons and bells. The sweet smell of incense and vanilla. The feel of fabric. Come experience Yellowgreen & Copper—a multi-sensory journal.

My first reaction to choosing a color was, "Oh boy, RED!" Then I thought, "NO, NO, NO! You always choose red. Here's the perfect opportunity to do something different, if not daring." Did I hurry up and choose something different? Nope. I shuffled around and stalled, and Sarah chose red! Then Teesha chose pink and orange. (Two colors! Oh my!) Two of my favorite colors were gone. I was up against a wall. I have an affinity with yellowgreen. Why not work with those shades? Yellowgreen reminds me of spring—tenderness, youth and new beginnings. The bright yellow lichen in the pine trees at Lake Wenatchee, and tightly coiled new sword ferns, and—oh joy—skunk cabbage. I love boggy places. Did you know that a skunk cabbage in the spring snow can actually heat up the area around it, melting the snow?

Copper was not new to me, but some of its uses in art journals were. My daughter Lesley and I had made books with copper covers in a workshop taught by Teesha and Tracy Moore. Then we took another class from Nina Bagley and Sarah Fishburn on journaling, where we saw neat jeweler's tricks that could be added to the books with copper tape, grommets and copper wire embellishments. So copper reminded me of some of the women I would be working with. Voila! I claimed Yellowgreen and Copper.
***
I wanted my pages to be loose, not bound in any way, to allow each person unlimited access to the page. No worries about getting someone else's pages sticky with paint, and you could work clear into the gutter of the pages even after the journal grew fat with additions of collaged stuff. I wanted the cover of my journal to be suspenseful, like opening a gift, or theatrical, like a stage presentation with curtains in between the acts. I hoped it would look interesting but not polished or intimidating. I was looking for something similar to some unfinished quilt pieces I have that date back to 1890. They are rough and ready—homespun-looking. I used a yellowgreen leopard stretch fabric on the inside and a subtle brown oak leaf and acorn print on the outside. I wanted to leave the material with rough edges but ended up doing a big buttonhole stitch on them.

***

I am not at all sure I can tell you in words how completely exhilarating it was working with this amazing group of women. I felt so energized and so challenged. The fact that they live all over the United States was intriguing in itself. Think about it: 16 journals traveling back and forth, back and forth across the continent. In the back of my mind, I was always aware of where the originator lived and curious about what subtle influences that might have on the work, maybe in colors, textures or content.

Each journal was so remarkably different, so captivating, that I felt I had to be on my toes, and open my heart to the wonder of it all. Just four of the women and the way they worked were known to me, so each time the mail carrier arrived with a new box it was, a "get ready" moment, a Christmas in April. One journal might be seductive, another whimsical, the next one a peek at days gone by. Occasionally, one would turn out to be an absolute dictator. "No, no, that won't do, start over!" The minute a new one arrived, I called up friends and said, "Drop everything and get over here quick to see this one!"

An extra dividend for participating in the project was being able to rave about the journals as they arrived with the 14 other players online. Sharing the cyber slices of "my life at this moment" added sweet and comforting human touches to the whole adventure. These are unstoppable, talented, dynamic women. I had to tap dance very fast to keep up, because each new journal was a completely new experience. It was a unique opportunity to be able to respond to someone else's artwork, to work with an array of materials in gorgeous colors and imagery. As the months went by, the ideas really began to percolate and spill over into my own artwork. Sometimes an idea for a journal page came immediately. Just a tiny item such as a button or a photo or a color would send a cascade of information that could be immediately put to use.

Occasionally there were so many possibilities it was hard to choose which one. At other times, nothing clicked until the last possible moment. The ultimate challenge was to be true to my own ideas and processes and to stay fresh. It was difficult not to be swept up into what other people had done. In retrospect, though, the hardest part of all was stopping—no more new journals to look forward to, and a brain still full of ideas. That was a sad day, mitigated only by the joyous arrival of my own journal, home for good.

—Linn C. Jacobs

Teesha Moore

Judi Riesch

Monica Riffe

Sarah Fishburn

Lisa Hoffman

Keely Barham

Linn Jacobs

Lynne Perrella

Marylinn Kelly

Claudine Hellmuth

Lisa Renner

Karen Michel

Michelle Ward

Anne Bagby

Artist: Linn C. Jacobs

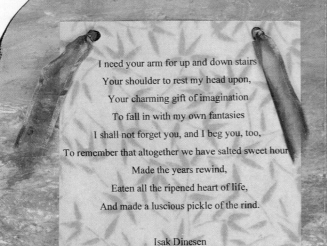

I need your arm for up and down stairs
Your shoulder to rest my head upon,
Your charming gift of imagination
To fall in with my own fantasies
I shall not forget you, and I beg you, too,
To remember that altogether we have salted sweet hour
Made the years rewind,
Eaten all the ripened heart of life,
And made a luscious pickle of the rind.

Isak Dinesen

Artist: Anne Bagby

I had misgivings when I read about these colors, but when the book arrived it was wonderful, the colors gorgeous. The layout of this book allowed me to leave it safely at home and work with my pages at my studio. These pages just developed on their own—it seemed like a profile was meant to be on the edge of the page, and that led to my drawing five profiles. If I ever do another swap like this, I want to do a similar layout. It is not a traditional book, but it is exciting to read, and it was great to work with.

—Anne Bagby

Artist: Lisa Renner

I knew immediately that I wanted to use metal surfacing products (Modern Options) to depict the colors Linn had selected. When I saw the format she had chosen, with the loose pages set inside a quadruple-fold portfolio, I came up with my entry. A piece of chipboard was cut to the appropriate size and green mulberry papers were glued to both sides. A piece of screen was sprayed with copper spray paint and folded into a pocket, then embellished with beads and wire. The screen pocket was attached to the mulberry base with brads. A simple book was made to slip inside the pocket. The covers of the book were treated with metal surfacing products in copper, rust and patina solutions. When they were dry, I rubbed green chalks into the patina to achieve the yellowgreen color.

—Lisa Renner

SPIRIT OF AUTUMN

A warm breeze floats
against the night
and mingles with the leaves
Creating sounds of magic,
to all that might believe
An illusion of stardust,
that glides to the ground

SONGBIRD

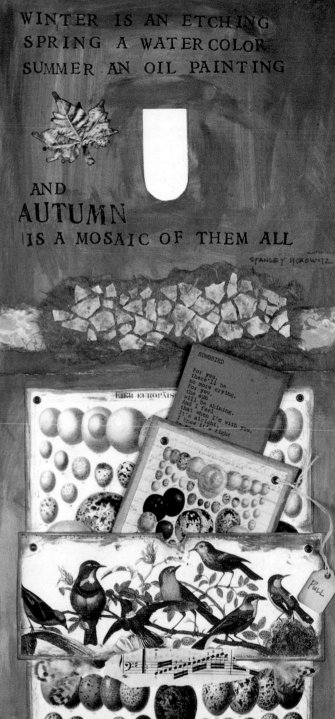

A creative offering of loose paper in a fabric enclosure, tied with ribbons and bells, Linn's journal announced liberty! To be able to work freely without the worry of messing up previous pages was a gift. I was also thrilled to work in my comfort palette. Because I learned Linn is an animal lover, I was tickled to find a quote about birds that also included autumn, my color choice. I knew right away that I would use my favorite "Songbird" by Eva Cassidy for a musical enclosure on a mini-CD. For the folded paper entry, I began with a doorway with a cut-out opening revealing a bird beyond on the next page. I used several prints of birds and eggs, attached with eyelets, creating placement for the CD and lyric enclosures. I enjoyed being able to work in this loose-page format, to be able to manipulate the layout by adding structure without feeling the guilt of imposing on the next artist's pages.

—Michelle Ward

Yellowgreen & Copper

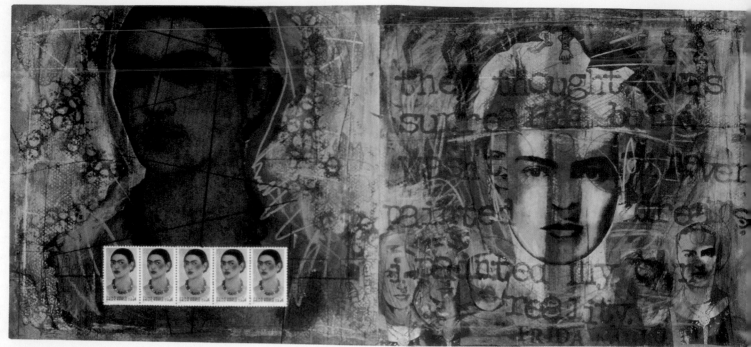

Yellowgreen & Copper

I can remember it very clearly. Linn's journal was not even out of the sealed carton and I was already savoring it. You see, it makes the most wonderful sound of temple bells. Inside the packing materials and tissue paper, it was shifting around, and the softly muffled sound of those lovely bells had me mesmerized—and ready to work. Once I had pulled the fabric-covered journal out of its wrappings, I could explore the multiple strands of ribbon ties and enjoy the scent of the vanilla sticks that Karen had incorporated into her entry. It was an experience of sights, sounds and smells heightened by Linn's unerring use of color. She is a Rainbow Wizard, someone who has a keen eye for placing strong colors together with ease—along with always knowing the best quotations on earth. It is her undisputed gift. I wanted to send Linn some pages about another wise woman who was savvy about color and wasn't afraid to push the creative envelope—Frida Kahlo. I wanted these pages to resemble some of the infamous self portraits done by Frida, where she stares out from the canvas, daring the world to understand her artwork.

—Lynne Perrella

Linn's journal was the first I received. I had never participated in a project like this and felt a bit adrift. Linn's sewn portfolio form made it easy to work on the pages, but because I was the first, I was not sure how much was enough. One of the gifts of this exchange was the realization that the only option was to press on regardless, no turning back. I fashioned some buttons out of shrink plastic, a favorite medium, and sewed a little pillow with an old photo transfer. As I reflected on my pages over the months of the project, they felt very scattered and unfocused. Because they were not bound in a book, Linn was able to send them back to me for a do-over. I saved pieces from the original pages and rearranged them in a similar but more pulled-together fashion. I added a quote from Ernest Holmen that reminded me of Linn as I had come to know her through months of correspondence: "Today I live in the quiet, joyous expectation of good."

—Marylinn Kelly

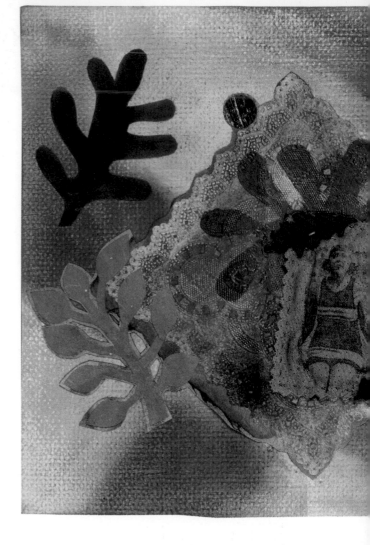

Artist: Sarah Fishburn

The work I did for Linn's journal was completed in the fall of 2001. It reflects the colors of autumn, including yellowgreen and copper, and the amazed innocence of a child seeing the world around him (for which inspiration I thank my own children and grandsons). Yet inside there's a short poem I wrote that is a melancholy remembrance of times past, never to be the same. I stamped it onto a page that I rolled with a brayer, over leaves that had fallen as I worked.

—Sarah Fishburn

TODAY I LIVE IN THE QUIET, JOYOUS EXPECTATION OF GOOD.
ERNEST HOLMES

WASHABLE BUTTONS

FOR SPORTS WEAR

Artist: Marylinn Kelly

Artist: Claudine Hellmuth

For Linn's journal, I created a fall-like piece using leaves and texts about leaves from an antique book. I was working on a similar design for a journal company, so I thought the Yellowgreen & Copper journal would be a good place to experiment. I also wanted to add beads and knick-knacks to the journal page like everyone else was doing, but in the past when I've tried this I never seemed to get the hang of it. This time I stitched on a few beads at the bottom of the page in colors that went with the leaf design. I liked the way it looked—it inspired me to think about using more beads in my artwork one day.

—Claudine Hellmuth

I really liked making the art quilt for Linn Jacob's journal. I loved the format of the loose pages. It meant I didn't have to glue my quilt down to a page—my work could be left free to be touched and felt, which is the whole joy of fabric things. I went through all of my printed fabric imagery, picking out things that were in the right color family. I sewed a backing fabric to each of them, then turned them right side out so all of the edges were finished. I then tucked them into layers of fabric so they moved freely except for the bottom edge. I hand-quilted all of the layers with embroidery floss and beads, then stem-stitched the words on the bottom layer.

—Keely Barham

They nicknamed it the Heavy Metal journal. Bigger than a phone book, and weighing a ton more, the Metallics journal impressed the artists by its sheer size and elegance. As Karen Michel notes, "This book evoked majesty."

For the journal's creator, Nina Bagley, the choice of color was a natural one. A jewelry artist, she was accustomed to working in metal. She made the journal from a vintage postcard album, embellishing the cover with a grid of 15 glass box tops filled with a variety of miniature images, including her mother and herself as an infant. Nina's golden memories.

Many artists felt the cover was a work of art in itself; a few were even intimidated to work in the book after seeing Nina's regal contribution. Inside, the journal is filled with all kinds of treasures. The artists used everything from precious gold leaf to common silver duct tape to answer the call for Metallics. All manifestations of metal can be found on its pages: milagros, charms, screens, grommets, plates—even a brass doorknocker. (No wonder it weighs so much!)

The artists' inventive use of found objects and lustrous, shimmering effects make the Metallics journal shine. You might say it's worth its weight in gold.

Metallics

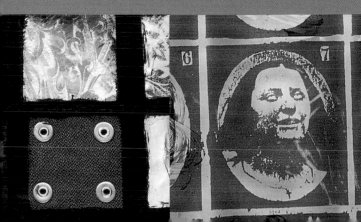

Golden crowns and halos.
Duct tape and tattered screens.
Things that are precious
and things discarded as "junk"
adorn the majestic Metallics journal.

ORIGINATING ARTIST:
Nina Bagley

At the onset of this wonderful project, headed by "the prism master" Lynne Perrella, a spectrum of colors was suggested somewhere in the beginning of an exciting flurry of e-mails amongst the 15 women selected for our collaboration. When classically-trained artist Lynne casually mentioned Metallics to me, knowing my jeweler's penchant for all things metal, I naturally jumped at the vision of bronze, silver, gold, and copper being shared with these other women. I've leaned heavily toward these neutral jeweler's colors with my design style all these years. Having worked as a metalsmith for 15 years, it seemed a natural progression to move toward the more subtle, patina-like shades of aged metals that would enhance delicate images pulled from vintage books and periodicals passed down to me from my father's demotion business findings. Lynne's keen sense of color and style matched my spirit; once I started the journal, I could not stop with one page. Nor two. Nor three! What innocently started as a simple color journal became affectionately dubbed by the color gals as Heavy Metal.

***

My choice for the journal was immediate: Straight from my stash of vintage books came a turn-of-the-century, well-loved, embossed black postcard album, very large, measuring 10"x15". The spine itself is a good 5 or 6 inches wide, accommodating marvelous heavy black pages with pre-cut slits for someone's collection of postcards. The album was empty and its corners were quite frayed (all the better) and faded from years of use and enjoyment. I decided to paint most of the album's front surface gold, and bordered the painted area with a vintage metal lampshade trim I unearthed in a salvage shop in Soho one wonderful snowy day long ago. Dividing the gold area into 15 sections, as a nod to our 15 artists, I embedded circular watch repair glass box tops that reveal assorted golden images. The central image is a chubby infant's face (mine, of course) with a crown atop her head. I'm flanked on my left by my favorite collage angel image holding a golden star. Below the angel is the man I like to think of as my muse, and below the muse are the arms of a clock reporting the time of 9 o'clock, a time that sounds like my name. Up on the right side, second from the top, is my mother as a young woman, another of my favorite images that I like to keep nearby.

From the start, I knew *True Colors* would be a unique experience, but little did I imagine the magnitude and impact it would gather as it spun its way through all of our lives. We all began thinking more "in color," and we chatted online about stocking up on imagery culled from various sources: flea markets, the Internet, magazine catalogs, recycled books. Drawers began to overflow with quite an array of rainbows, and in my color stash, this was an oddity. Try as I might to branch out, my usual choices tend to limit themselves to the classic neutral tones of sepias, blacks, and creams, highlighted by my jeweler's penchant for all things metal—copper, brass, bronze, silver, gold. This, then, was my first challenge. Color! I shuddered when trying to imagine the first attempts at working a page in something other than what I normally created in my little studio. Yet when the first journal arrived, it was much easier than I anticipated to plunge in with Anne Bagby's color choice of yellow and violet. The words were easy, the images even easier. So it began, and I saw a very fine pattern in myself emerging, one of an artist and her stories.

As time passed, I began to have more difficulties with what I considered a constricted time schedule (having to send one journal on its way every two weeks). The project began in the summer, and I was in the midst of travel and the comings and goings of my teenaged boy, as well as trying to meet deadlines in my work and other art. At one point I looked at my studio side table and saw three or four journals sitting untouched, and felt the heavy weight of guilt and responsibility for an entire group bearing down. I decided it wouldn't be fair to everyone else to be consistently late with the journals. I wrote the group, explained my situation and extreme regrets, but felt that the best situation would be for me to bow out. The general feeling of the group was one of graciousness, understanding and support, I suppose because they are women who all juggle commitments at home and at work—children, art, career—and could certainly understand my need to prioritize. In the end, they rallied together and chose to include me anyway, sending my Heavy Metal behemoth back and forth to everyone in the group and inviting me to make art pages in their journals when my schedule lightened up and time permitted. The group is a lovely, familial one—beautiful women who understand and encourage one another openly. For that I am grateful, and feel that we've all grown in ways that reach far beyond art techniques and paper surfaces.

—Nina Bagley

...pe is the thing with

feathers

that

perches in

the soul

look closely

I will alway...

...part of it...

...the wa...

...es is proof...

...epths...

Judi

Monica

...ANDOM TH...

Y SARAH...

OCTOBER

...E TH...

Sarah

Michele

510

it's good to be queen

...airy Tale for a

YES

...watched them

And at last one came up, bi...

...and stopp...

ju·mi·nous

...xious and

...g another

...had not

but was... silver

"My d...

"you really...

Artist: Nina Bagley

This book was a challenge, not only because of the oversized pages, which made it hard to keep the book propped open, but because the pre-cut slits in the paper required some problem-solving. I tackled these issues by adding elements over the pages. For the first entry, I used huge grommets to attach several pages together to create a stable foundation. Brass mesh was mounted with eyelets, then a real brass door knocker was wired on with brass wings. The quote was stamped with gold paint.

For the next entry, I painted with metallic silver and gold and added a Madonna image transfer with stamped designs to create a shrine, then mounted a collection of silver and gold religious medals.

The last entry focused on a favorite quote (from a Girl Scouts song): "Make new friends, but keep the old; one is silver and the other gold." I felt this was an appropriate quote for the journal because it mentions the precious metals and it represented this project, where we made some new friends. One page is a grid of applied papers and elements in silver. The following page was done with the same techniques in gold.

—Michelle Ward

I was completely blown away by Nina's journal. I couldn't believe it when I opened the box. It was a complete work of art on its own, and I had no idea how to add to it. Nina had earmarked several pages for each of us to work on, a challenge in itself, so I did my best to fill them.

—Keely Barham

SCOOP UP
WATER,
THE MOON
IS IN YOUR
HANDS

I remember taking Nina's Metallics book to a party where there was a bunch of artist friends. Everyone's reaction to this book was the same: awe. The size of this journal is big, like Nina's heart. And the interactive details, such as the words tucked into lockets, or the Random Words page where we were encouraged to leave notes, were so fun. At first, I was daunted by her request to create four pages, but they filled up surprisingly fast. I even did a colored pencil drawing, which for me was risk-taking.

—Monica Riffe

Metallics

Metallics usually conjure up images of gold, silver and bronze. I took a slightly different direction and used metallic colors instead. First, I sponged metallic acrylic paints onto pieces of joss paper. Next, I glued the paper onto the pages so they slightly overlapped. The female image was enlarged, mounted onto mat board and cut out. Gold leaf was added to the doll's hat and amber gems simulated the "crushed diamonds" in her eyes. The poem was one I started about a year ago, but thought it appropriately illustrated my Metallics page.

—Lisa Renner

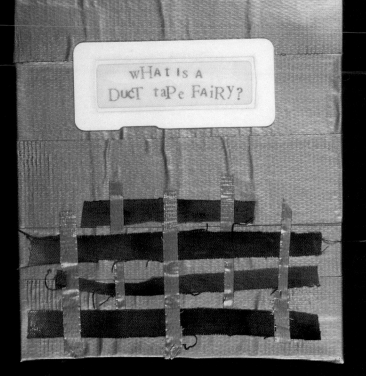

Just the act of hoisting this book onto a table was an experience! This journal was big, beautiful and powerful. My reaction had a lot to do with the need to make a statement that echoed the magic of the work, while tossing in a liberal dose of mischief. Thus, The Duct Tape Fairies were born.

I had to create their story visually and quickly, so I decided to do a written "Profile." These are the fairies that your mama did NOT want whispering ideas in your ear, so I gave the pages a rough, "street-y" look. The description was to appear as though it had been scraped off the ground in an alley, so I actually balled up the paper and walked on it with my kicker-boots! I used strips of ripped muslin, dipped in a black watercolor bath, which contrasted with the silver metallic duct tape.

The Duct Tape Fairies' photos were chosen to be consistent with the image of sexy, street-smart and just a little dangerous. I hoped that Nina would be amused with the journey into the wild side of what I picture to be her beautiful world, filled with things of a gentle, lovely and mysterious nature.

—Lisa Hoffman

This amazing behemoth from Nina Bagley arrived just before I left on a car trip to Eureka, California, for a book-making workshop. The cover is a work of art that can stand alone (literally), and when you open the book up, well, it is perfect. I dragged the journal along with me to the workshop to give it a wider audience. We photographed it in the motel room, on the beach, and in a dry golden grassy field just north of the California border. In Eugene, I found the perfect beaded fringe in silvery metallic for it.

For weeks, I had the little brass grasshopper and some silver stars waiting in the wings for the book to arrive. One of the things Nina occasionally says is "grasshoppa" (from the TV show Kung Fu). But I misplaced the stars before the journal made it to Tacoma. The pages were of a delicate black paper, so I glued two together for mine, and there were lots and lots of pages, so I got a little carried away. I think I even stitched around the edges of two or more.

For my entry, I used my big antique silver paper fan and multiples of the same 1800 Native American princess image. It was hard to work in the gutter in this journal—it was so fat!

—Linn C. Jacobs

Metallics

I was the last artist to work in the unique and wonderful Metallics journal, and I was in awe of the work that came before me. This was one instance where all my gathering of "stuff" ahead of time didn't matter. Any previous notions of a plan for this journal went right out the window. I allowed the creative juices to percolate for a few days, then I began my entry by gluing several of the pages together. Pre-cut slits used for sliding in an old postcard collection were making the pages too fragile.

The journal's large format was a little intimidating, so I painted the black pages with wide streaks of gold. I added a touch of metal with a tintype photo of a young girl and lots of German embossed foil die-cuts. I plucked the sweet ballerina from my collection of dancing girls and placed her on a starry stage, a marionette of the night. Photo album pages created a window to "preview" the Dance by the Light of the Moon.

—Judi Riesch

I had heard the buzz that Nina's heavily embellished and festooned book was heav-y, baby, heav-y. I was delighted to find out why. When I hoisted it out of its carton, I began to appreciate the reason for all that weightiness and plot my own addition to the large black pages.

I had recently come across an old archival image of a series of photos depicting facial studies and found it oddly narrative and compelling. At a glance, it seemed to be just another series of posed head shots of some nameless Victorian lady, but a closer look revealed a more scholarly presentation of the various muscles of the face and how they work. I found it interesting that early photography would be put to such a fascinating use, and decided to combine this with clip art images of jewels.

Next to the human face, the perfect jewels seemed, well, too perfect. And the humanity of the woman sitting for the photographs seemed to shine forth. The use of "paper jewels" was a way to contrast with the lovely handmade and expertly fashioned metal delights that Nina had made for her journal. The jewels on my pages were momentary and pretend, while Nina's ability as a jeweler is allowed to shine for real.

—Lynne Perrella

Metallics

There was quite a buzz going around about this book. Whenever someone received, it she would check in with an e-mail that could generally be summarized as "Wowza!" Let me tell you, wowza was right. The box itself was huge, and a slight jingle could be heard when shaking it. Opening the box was like unearthing a lost treasure. I carefully lifted out the journal and examined every detail of every page like an archeologist on a very important excavation.

As far as inspiration goes, this book evoked majesty. It was an antique photo album, so the challenge was to work around the pre-cut page slits for photos. For each page, I placed a strip of masking tape over the slits, primed the pages with gesso, then applied a layer of iridescent gold. I used the same technique on all three spreads, unifying my work in this journal.

—Karen Michel

Michelle Ward chose the most colorful time of the year for her palette—Autumn. Instead of limiting themselves to one or two colors, the artists were free to work in red, rust, mustard, copper, brown, and green tones. Michelle added a novel feature to the Autumn journal that the artists loved: She created a sign-in page based on the "The Princess and the Pea" fairytale, making a stack of "mattresses" out of paper in shades that corresponded to the colors the artists chose for their journals. Each artist signed her tag and inserted it into her designated mattress, then went to work on her entry.

Many chose themes for their Autumn pages that reflected the transitory nature of the season. Lisa Hoffman used seashells and pearls—not fallen leaves—to frame an old photograph of a turn-of-the-century beauty. Judi Riesch chose the theme of school days of the past, remembering how it felt to head back to class in new clothes, ready for the coming year.

As the days shorten and shadows lengthen, fall is a time for contemplating things that have transpired and things to come. Marylinn Kelly writes, "Doing these Autumn pages was a form of time travel, a journey back to retrieve moments whose meaning grows with the years."

Autumn

A season to be savored. A magic
time of warm, rich hues.
Autumn, like youth,
ends all too soon,
so linger over
these journal pages.

By the time I had to settle on a color, more than half of our group had already made their color selections. I was torn between claiming sage or copper, two of my favorites. Then it occurred to me to be clever and announce Autumn—not a color, but a range of colors. To me, Autumn meant green, gold, red, rust, mustard, copper, and brown. It felt like cheating to claim a season, but it also felt so right.

Autumn is the most glorious time of year, when the air changes in relief from summer heat. The leaves reveal their handsome tricks and neighborhoods are filled with color. For some, the season may symbolize the beginning of an end, but to me it actually means new beginnings. With fall comes a new school year, which means new clothes and shoes, fresh notebooks, sharpened pencils, and brand new crayons. More importantly, there's so much to learn, and new friendships to be made. Choosing Autumn as my journal color meant I was providing a book that could be home to a variety of color interpretations. And this collaborative project ended up being like school, where I definitely learned about myself, about style, about technique, and about color. I also made many new girlfriends.

***

For the Autumn journal, I chose a spiral-bound book with a sage and gold harlequin patterned cover. The cover colors influenced my applied design of a copied book cover with gold trim, coffee-dyed paper, old text, and a stamped image of a tree. I added oak leaf charms, letting the glue ooze out, and applied Pearl-Ex. With the first few finished pages, I wanted to convey that Autumn meant many colors.

My favorite entry is the sign-in page. When I was browsing through special Autumn-toned papers, it occurred to me to use all of them and create a stack of mattresses, as in the fairytale about the princess and the pea. Each paper selection was attached with a slide-out slot for each artist to register. I arranged the mattresses so the color would reflect, not only my Autumn palette, but a close representation of the individual artists' chosen color as well.

***

Being part of this collaboration was both a privilege and a thrill, especially because I was new to art journals. It terrified me to jump into such an extensive project, yet I knew it would be a tremendous learning experience. It was validating as an artist to be included on Lynne's list of participants, and her invitation alone gave me confidence that I had something to offer.

While I attempted to think ahead and plan for each journal's arrival, I ended up changing direction after being influenced by each book itself or the entries preceding mine. The only downside was letting go of a journal when I would have preferred to have it visit me a little longer. As each volume entered my studio, it contained more entries than the previous one and obviously carried a deeper meaning.

In addition to being challenged with a different color each round, I found that working in another artist's journal brought me to a new level of art. For me, there was a self-imposed responsibility to create pages that fit the style of the book, that carried meaning.

—Michelle Ward

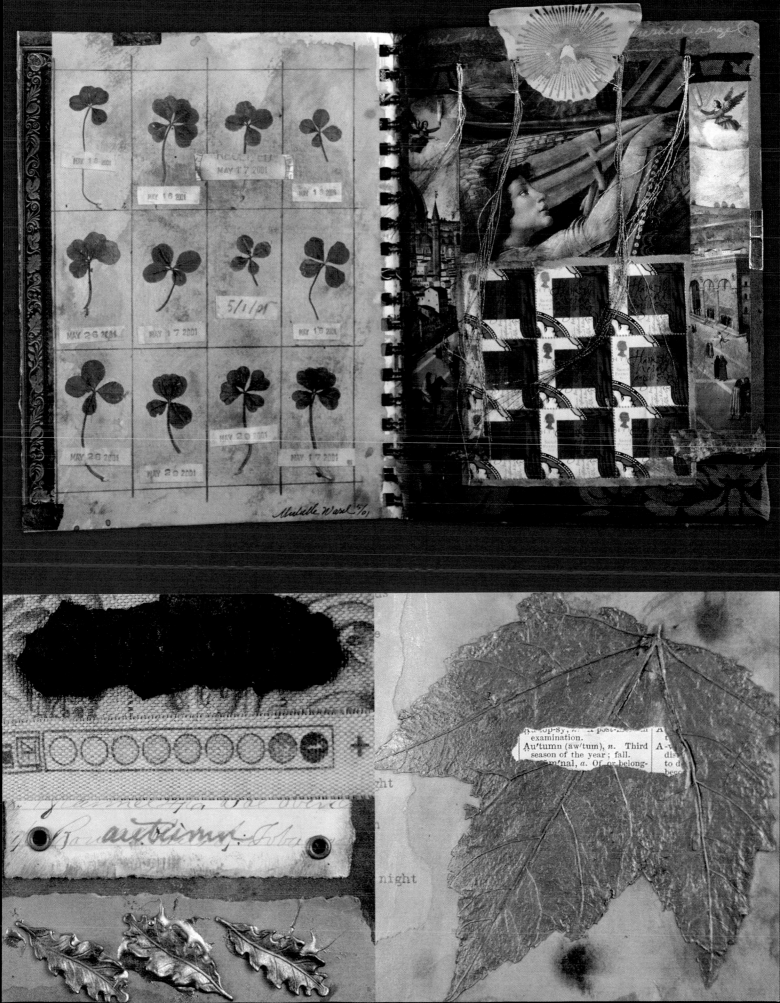

Artist: Michelle Ward

Autumn

Artist: Keely Barham

I chose a clock/time theme with the words "Time Flies" for the Autumn journal because, to me, the season just flies by and it's winter before you know it. I stamped the letters on fabric and cut them out. I collaged and sewed all of the fabric imagery, leaves cut from a commercial fabric and clocks onto brown handmade paper. I also added a paper pouch that I sewed together and put a quilted leaf inside.

—Keely Barham

I envisioned a purple and gold color theme for the Autumn journal. I pictured brittle leaves blowing across the sky in a crisp wind. I used purple, gold and ochre acrylic paints over the pages, applying the paint with a brayer. The inside page is watercolor paper slathered with gel medium. I pressed skeleton leaves into the gel while it was wet. When dry, I painted the surface with the same colors. Highlights were added with Rub 'n Buff.

—Lisa Renner

Artist: Lisa Renner

Artist: Monica Riffe

I have an ancient bottle of gesso that is going dry. Instead of throwing it out, I developed a technique where I spread some of the thick gooey gesso onto a page, then close the book so that it transfers some gesso to the opposite page. This makes a textural surface that looks like stucco. I like the way it holds rubbed-in color and has a luminous quality, like a sun-drenched fall day.

—Monica Riffe

Michelle was such an amazing contributor. She made a CD of the perfect musical accompaniment for each journal—imagine. She also made a page of stamps from each of our journal covers. I was inspired by Claudine and her figure in the photo album archway; it reminded me of the three cherubs, and the symbolism of three things is something Claudine talked about in her slide lecture at ArtFest. The next spread of two similar pages was one of my favorite entries—oak leaves, sunflowers on fabric, snippets of actual sunflower photos, along with buttons, threads and "hidden" quotes.

—Linn C. Jacobs

Artist: Linn C. Jacobs

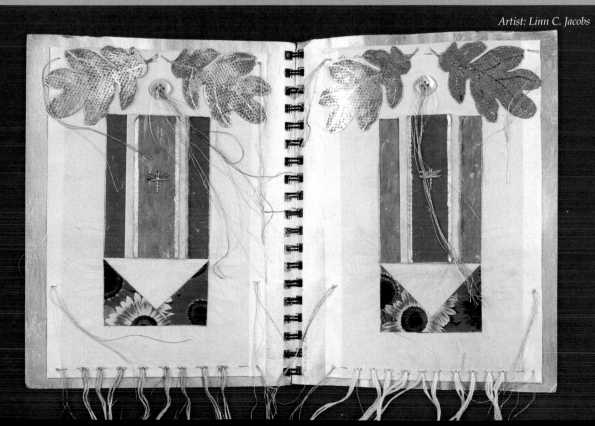

Autumn was my first book. The beauty of Michelle's work was rather intimidating, but I was pleased with my poem—it seemed to fit—and I had a good time stamping it from different alphabets. Michelle's book had a theme for each color, but she made it clear what colors we were to use.

My turn followed Michelle's throughout the entire project, and she always had wonderful pages. One of the joys of this book swap was seeing her work. She produced consistently high-quality pages, and she always included a tag or a gift and a note for me. It was great meeting her this way, and even better when we met in person at "the gathering." There are not many people as much fun or as generous with her ideas and talents as Michelle. I felt lucky to be her "partner" in this project.

—Anne Bagby

Artist: Teesha Moore

I was not inspired by the Autumn journal. Anything with brown in it just holds no interest for me. While I love the season immensely, the colors seem boring. I guess I was trying (a little too much) to punch it up, so I got out my "Autumn"-colored glitter paint and went to town.

Autumn is the time for Halloween, and I suppose that inspired the artwork. In the same vein as others before me, I tried adding yarn and doodads but failed in my attempts to do it with style. I was trying to do it in another style (not my own) and just made a mess.

—Teesha Moore

Ah! Relief! Autumn was easy, with its hints of my palette of bronzes and coppers and all that is golden and sepia. Michelle's large pages were an open door for me to dive in with reckless abandon, with little wooden picket fences, vintage sepia photographs, pearl buttons, and my standard use of tarnished copper tape. Michelle and I have shared our penchant for all things centered on the theme of home, and I used this theme for her pages. I stamped the words "please come home" under a vintage photograph of a woman standing in front of her house, at the steps, as if waiting for her beloved to return. Here's to home, Michelle, and the love that we both share for ours!

—Nina Bagley

Artist: Nina Bagley

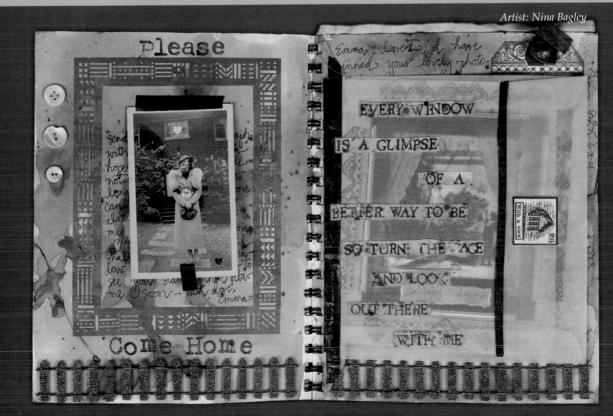

No. 85. AUTUMN WINDS ARE SIGHING.

A
B C
D E
F
G H I

teacher

MADE IN
U.S.A.

school days

school-book (skool'book')
school-boy (skool'boi'), n., a boy
school-fel-low attends school.
school-girl (skool'fel'o), n., a com-
school-house panion at school.
school-ing (skool'girl'), n., a girl who
elpline; reproof; attends school.
(skool'hous'), n., a build
school-man where school is held
divines or philosophers (skool'ing), n. 1, instruction
school-mas-ter school; education; 2, d
(skool'man'), n. (pl. scho
school-mate (skool'mas'ter), one of
school-room the head or principal of a s
school-teach-er (skool'mat'), n. a
(skool'mis'tress'),

Autumn

Artist: Judi Riesch

No. 85. AUTUMN WINDS ARE SIGHING.

I loved receiving Michelle's journal, its Autumn theme being close to my heart. Having an October birthday, fall has always been my favorite time of year, and I was torn between two ideas that represent the season to me: school days and Halloween. I decided to do both and began with school days, remembering a song my mother used to sing about "Dear Old Golden Rule Days." I was saving some marbled end papers from an old book in gorgeous shades of sage greens, golden ochres and deep wines, and they became the base for my pages. Inside an accordion book I fashioned from old book covers is a collection of 1930s school

photos and snippets from a penmanship notebook. The requisite numbers and letters were made with punches and stencils. I couldn't help but smile at Anna, the be-ribboned young girl in the photo above the book. She reminds me of myself during those September days, plaid jumper and all, ready to start school fresh and new. I had this journal for a while and needed to move it on its journey, so the Halloween spread had to be put on hold. I reserved my space, however, by claiming two pages in my name, so I could be sure to have this book back again.

—Judi Riesch

Autumn

Michelle's book was to die for. In the front, she had all these tassels where each artist could sign off that she had worked in the book. I couldn't get over what a great idea that was. I never thought to have a place in my journal where other artists could leave messages. For Michelle's journal, I continued my obsession with tintype frames and used an old frame as a centerpiece for a very simple collage. I loosely painted a green background, then assembled the entire collage on top.

—Claudine Hellmuth

During an early morning walk, I realized that the small pointed golden leaves I was admiring were from a willow tree. Willow. Michelle lives on Willow Avenue. She and I share an enjoyment of Paul McCartney's music and one of my favorite McCartney tunes is "Little Willow." It was all coming together.

I remembered that one of the first conversations I had with Michelle was about tag art, so I decided to use some tags to house the leaves, some transparencies of nudes, and some sepia-toned stampings. She loves architecture and is a skilled draftsperson, so I added some Xerox transfers of windows and doorways.

For the final page, I made a booklet with a ribbon tie to hold the song lyrics and thought my entry was complete. One night, I sat with the book in my lap, appreciating the fire in the hearth. I jumped up, lit one of the long fireplace tapers, and touched it to the edges of the journal. The heavy painted pages smoldered and the flames nibbled at the edges, making curves like the shape of fall leaves.

—Lynne Perrella

Artist: Claudine Hellmuth

Artist: Lynne Perrella

Most important of all should be your
kind to all living things both great and

piness into the world. Make yours a world of joy and
freedom for "all things growing"!

These pages were made with a lot of love. Michelle was the person who received my journals after I worked on them. We would e-mail often and sometimes talk and send one another music. I felt close to her because her husband is a musician and mine is, too. She has so many children of her own, roundabout and underfoot, and I have had that as well in my life.

The music part of our relationship is reflected in the two pages on which I printed the beautiful lyrics of the Johnny Mercer classic, "Autumn Leaves," and on the facing free spirit pages. The images of the little boys are from a beautiful old photograph I have; I used them to illustrate the role of children in our lives. The buttons holding the gingham ribbon in place all have fall motifs and were my great-gram's.

—Sarah Fishburn

and helps all trees. Be kind! Preach kindr
associates. Kindness brings love and beau

1. Collect pictures of the moon, birds, insects, trees, and animals. Paste them in your scrapbook.

trees are

I have found that, although the lowly insect does great harm to trees, yet it is food for the bird who befriends

play

sf 2002 sf 2002

2. Make a sketch of the locust tree. In an insert draw the leaf.

The leaves of the locust tree are oval from one to two inches in length. rounded. There are leaf stalk, an

I took texture to the next level on this one. After seeing an amazing book on sailors valentines, I decided to give the technique a try. I used a ton of little shells and a bag of seed pearl beads that I happened to have lying around. A big piece of rusted cable acts like a border between the outside of the frame and the image. The wonderful picture had just the right touch of whimsy and fun. The outside of the frame is bordered by four sticks that I wired onto mat board. The copy portion of the layout is an entry from my diary, written when I was in London in the '70s. I knew that Michelle's husband is British, so I enjoyed tossing that in. I built up the layers by mounting a huge shell between the layers of board. There is a shell just under the poem that stands proudly on a rusted metal heart.

—Lisa Hoffman

Season Three

We knew that Autumn would still bring the Sun.

It felt wiser, with a richness and strength,

having lived through a virginal Spring

and reveled in the passionate touch

of an experienced Summer.

The London Journals-Saint Johns Wood 1976

There's something decidedly feminine about the Violet & Yellow journals. The tall, narrow shape of the books and the sweet, spring-like colors prompted many of the artists to fill the journals with female images. Bathing beauties, girls in white dresses and assorted maidens adorned the artists' pages. Marylinn Kelly was reminded of her grandmother, who loved violets. There was, she wrote, "something quiet and gentle about the books."

Anne Bagby created the Violet & Yellow journals as three books-in-a-box because she wanted to give the artists enough space; they were free to work in one book or all three, and they could create horizontal or vertical layouts. Anne prepped the pages of the coil-bound journals with paint, gesso, tissue paper, and other materials to jump-start the artists' creativity. Most loved the journals' format and textured paper, and soon the books outgrew their original box.

When her journals came back to Anne, they were filled with flowers; the artists decorated their work with pansies, violets and daisies. Her journals even smelled like flowers, courtesy of Michelle Ward, who gave them a proper sendoff complete with a bigger wooden box, lavender confetti and the scent of violets. Sweet and sentimental—that's Violet & Yellow.

Violet &

Yellow

Pansies in springtime.
Fair maidens, geishas and
winged angels.
Like these lovely creatures,
the Violet & Yellow journals
give pleasure to all
who gaze upon them.

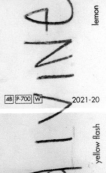

ORIGINATING ARTIST:
Anne Bagby

The *True Colors* project gave me the opportunity to get to know the other artists and see what they did in the journals. I was amazed that each book seemed to have a separate personality that strongly suggested, if not what I should do, then what I shouldn't do for its pages. It is very different working in someone else's journal instead of my own. The color I chose for my journal was even different for me. I chose purple because Lynne had pointed out earlier that I hated purple. I thought that I shouldn't hate a primary color when there are only six of them.

As soon as I started covering the watercolor paper I used for the book with paint, I knew purple was a good choice. I liked the subtle color combinations violet and yellow made. I used coil-bound books because, although I wanted a handmade book, I don't know how to do regular binding. The three books are figure-shaped, in keeping with my private promise to work with a figure on these books. I started three so the artists would have enough pages to work on. I didn't anticipate that the books would grow too big for the box. Michelle Ward found the second box that just fit and protected the books. I might have planned differently if I had realized how delicate my books would be, but I was pleased with how they looked when finished.
***
I decided to make the *True Colors* project as much of a learning tool as possible. Every page would have a figure in it, and I would sew (something new for me–I just got a sewing machine) on each page. Although other ideas took precedence on some books (a figure wasn't appropriate or there wasn't enough time to do any sewing), for the most part I was able to practice these new skills and produce some good work.

My work is usually formed by slowly layering until I produce something I like, so the prospect of completing a page to send in just two weeks was sort of scary (and

did indeed prove difficult). I tried to work on my pages in advance, but when the books arrived they always seemed to call for something different than what I had prepared. Through the process, I learned to simply prepare several pieces of colored, patterned and textured paper and to collect things in the chosen color, rather than plan a theme.
***
I think we all realized from the start that this project was special. It was a real bonding experience. Each of us put forth our best and tried to do something spectacular on each page. Although most of us were strangers, we recognized the names of the other artists on the list and felt like we were in exalted company. I had not been working in books for very long and knew I would have to hustle to keep up.

While worrying about my own performance, I didn't give the final Violet & Yellow books much thought. I felt as though the outcome of projects like this can often be disappointing. I wanted to make the creation of the pages themselves the most important part of the project. That way, no matter how my books turned out, I would feel my time was well invested. I was not particularly excited about the return of my box—I was prepared to be "under-whelmed" (although I had seen the other books and knew how great they were).

I was very surprised at my reaction when my three little books came home and I saw them complete for the first time. Michelle Ward prepared the package with bows and confetti and the smell of violets. I immediately loved them. One of the things I love about art books is how personal they are, and this collection of books is the most personal I have ever had. My journal seemed to embody pieces of the heart of each of the participants. Every time I turn the pages, I am flooded with emotion.
—Anne Bagby

Artist: Judi Riesch

Violet & Yellow

I was crazy about Anne's color choices and her format. When I saw these books, I couldn't choose between the horizontal and vertical formats, so I decided to do two pages in each style. They are some of my favorite pages for True Colors; *the 4"x10" size is so cool and appealing. The handmade paper Anne bound into the books was groovy for getting started—I love incorporating ready-made backgrounds with my own work.*

I adore flower names for girls—my oldest daughter is September Rose. When I began the vertical pages, I knew that Violet was the perfect name for one little girl and my all-time favorite, Daisy, would be her friend.

—*Sarah Fishburn*

Artist: Sarah Fishburn

Violet & Yellow

Anne's small books and the box she created to hold them were so charming. My favorite spread that I did in her journal was the Japanese geisha girl that I drew and painted with watercolor over some background stamping of Japanese calligraphy.

—Keely Barham

Anne's journals were the last ones I received. I loved her format of creating these spiral-bound books made with her own painted patterns and additional specialty papers. I chose to complete several journal entries to fill in the spaces left in the books. Some were done in yellow, some in violet, and some in a combination of the two colors. For one spread, I played off the tune "Bicycle Built for Two" using daisies, tandem bicycles, a packet of daisy seeds, and enclosed lyrics to the song. For another entry, I chose a story about starfish and created a mini-booklet to hold the text, and I found an old postcard of a bathing beauty with a sunset in violet and yellow. I enjoyed playing with purple and yellow paint on a two-page spread in one of Anne's journals, adding a favorite quote to one and an old postcard and fabric swatch to the other. On another two-page spread, I used purple and teal paint with metallic gold and added stamped items to complete the pages. I compiled a list of songs on a mini-CD to accompany Violet & Yellow, but I couldn't find a recording of "Bicycle Built for Two." After working in Anne's journals, I found myself drawn to using purples in my own work.

—Michelle Ward

Clockwise from upper left: Michelle Ward,
Keely Barham and Michelle Ward

Artist: Monica Riffe

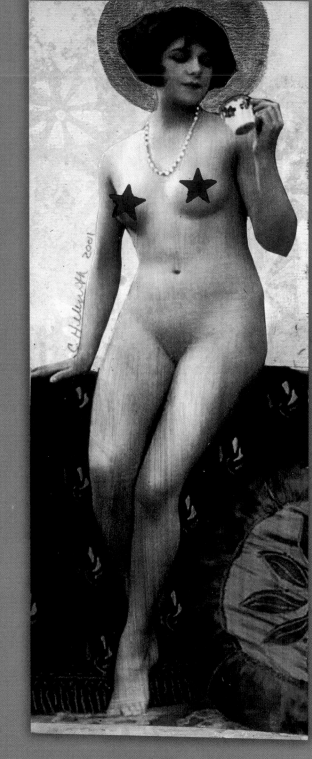

Artist: Claudine Hellmuth

"Three's a charm." That saying fits Anne's books, nestled in their box. Inside, the adorned handmade pages were almost too beautiful to alter. The inclusion of Lynne's violet glasses doubled the fun. At the end of the project, Anne made a gift of a pair of violet plastic scissors. It was the surprise and delight at opening each **True Colors** package that, to me, captures the essence our project.

—Monica Riffe

Anne's journals arrived in a long, thin box that she had collaged and designed. She had three slender journals in the box for us to work in. I really liked the format of her books, and I decided to do a standing figure because she fit the shape of the book. I was really moved by Anne's artwork. I love her technique of drawing into her collages, and seeing these journals started me thinking about incorporating more drawing into my own collages.

—Claudine Hellmuth

Artist: Keely Barham

Artist: Teesha Moore

Anything with yellow is a turn-on for me, and the two colors immediately got me excited. I also loved the size of this long, narrow journal. I had Nina's Metallics journal and Anne's journal in my possession at the same time, so I used a few of the same materials on both journals. Some fabrics in my stash screamed to be used in Anne's journal, so that set the tone for my entry. The journal size was perfect to go under the needle of my sewing machine. I prefer sewing or any other kind of attachment to glue. It's just so messy. The images I used were color copies of parts of my own journal.

—Teesha Moore

Artist: Nina Bagley

Artist: Nina Bagley

Violet & Yellow

I've always incorporated a tiny story line in my art journal pages, whether through the use of simple imagery and succession of emotion behind the pictures submerged in my pages or with the addition of subtle words of my own. This happened with Anne's pages, and was a natural flow for each and every one of the other journals to follow. In rifling through my very messy drawers for bits and pieces of appropriate color, I came up with butterflies and kings. Ah. The Butterfly Kings. The rest was simple.
—Nina Bagley

Artist: Sarah Fishburn

Violet & Yellow

When Anne's Violet & Yellow journal arrived, I was
delighted to have a choice of three different books in which
to work. This clever lady provided spiral-bound books she
fashioned out of specialty papers as well as papers she
created with her hand-carved images. These instant
backgrounds made for an easy beginning, and I had already
collected an array of appropriate papers, trims and paints.
As I worked on more and more of the journals, it became
more natural for me to work with color. I actually began to
look forward to the challenge of a new palette. The tall, thin
pages of the Violet & Yellow books lent themselves well to
images of young girls, and my focus became the fragility of
youth. I used an abundance of dried pansies—the flower of
youth—and applied them with a gel medium that created a
kind of translucent quality. I enjoyed working in this
smaller format and made a note to myself to start a mini
journal. The idea of using a coil binding and hand-selecting
papers was terrific.

—Judi Riesch

DAISY
DAISY

you'll look sweet
upon the seat
of a bicycle
built for two

Daisy Bell

59

Artist: Karen Michel

Artist: Linn C. Jacobs

This was a little box of gems. Looking through these books, I wasn't sure which one I wanted to work on—each book and page was so carefully prepared.

—Karen Michel

Anne's Violet & Yellow journal is another one of my favorites. The format is three wonderfully tall and skinny books. Her technique with paint and gesso and stencils/stamps is masterful, and the colors are perfect together. So what to do, what to do? I started with Claudine's imagery, because by now I was totally keyed into what she was doing. Next, I was smitten with Nina's story of the Butterfly Kings and dreamed up a story line about the monkey ruler with feathers for the book pages.

—Linn C. Jacobs

Artist: Michelle Ward

Artist: Linn C. Jacobs

Artist: Lynne Perrella

I loved Anne's little box-of-books. At the heart of it, Anne is a teacher as well as an artist. This was reflected in the way she had carefully prepped each and every page of the blank journals with base coats of tissue paper, gesso and other favored techniques that Anne uses to make her pages so full of depth and underlying texture. We were all treated to the experience of a starting point that was already vastly interesting, thanks to Anne. I admire what Anne does, and I like the strong signature of her work, although she is always learning and expanding her vocabulary. I wanted my pages in her book to have a feeling of continuity and tunnel-like passages, so I planned them with lots of see-through elements and structural references that would give a sense of a tour through a fortress or castle.

—Lynne Perrella

Karen Michel's Violet & Green journal invoked the spirits of Jack Kerouac, '60s gurus, Indian mystics and magicians. Lynne Perrella writes: "Karen's journal looked like it could have easily spilled right out of Jack's rucksack, like a mystic volume containing notes, secrets, poems, and prayers."

Karen encouraged the artists to express their spiritual natures by fearlessly experimenting with color and materials. She set the tone by making her journal out of two children's books, lashing the covers together with twine and coloring them with a thick layer of gesso and watercolor crayon. She playfully stapled a heart to the inside cover and colored a childlike handprint on the facing page. In an e-mail to the other artists, Karen called hearts and hands "beautiful archetypes that link us all together."

The artists responded to her invitation to play by trying all kinds of techniques with fabric, corrugated cardboard, stickers, transparencies, bottle caps, a rusty nail, fiber—even a razor blade. Michelle Ward got into the spirit by attaching a denim pocket to her page that she stuffed with Pop Rocks candy.

As Lynne put it in an e-mail: "Karen's journal pages are perfect reminders to me: Get messy! Load up the page with stuff! Throw on more and more and more layers! Glue things down, and paint over 'em!" In short, the artists used their hands—and their hearts.

Violet & Green

Dominoes take flight.
Girls sport angels' wings.
A magical,
transcendental experience.
A journal where
anything can happen.

For me, violet is the highest of colors. It is associated with the crown chakra (one of the body's energy points, each being associated with a color), that represents thought, understanding and transcendence. It was also my favorite color as a child.

Green is pure earth energy, the color of trees and grass from spring through summer—fresh, clean and full of life. Green is associated with the heart chakra, which represents love, breath, unity and healing. Joining these two colors together for this project felt right—a joining of the spirit and the earth within the pages of my own personal playground, which would be shared with fellow artists whose work I admired greatly.
***
I knew when I began constructing my book that it would need some good solid "road legs" because it would be-bop from coast to coast. Fragile just would not do. So I took the hard covers of two children's books, sewed them together with some twine, and primed them with a few good layers of gesso. Going for simplicity, I colored in the cover with a violet watercolor crayon and added a sweet little embroidered violet patch from India that I had been saving for a special occasion.
***
After binding the book and creating the first and last page, I simply placed it in a soft priority mail envelope because it was quite flat. When the journal came back home, I found it wrapped in soft green paper, tied with a violet ribbon, adorned with a soft pink velvet rose and placed within a deep, well-worn cardboard box to protect its now busting

pages. A truly royal homecoming. For the rediscovery of my well-traveled creation, I conducted my ceremony of tea and art table preparation. But this time around I had a Jack Kerouac spoken word CD from Lynne, a magical necklace to wear from Nina and the hearts and souls of all my new friends within its luscious pages.
***
When I was invited to participate in this project, I was flattered. I found myself surrounded by artists I greatly admired, whose work would be bound within my book and mine within theirs. Never one for being good with a deadline, however, the thought of turning over a book every two weeks and mailing it off to the next artist on time made me a bit nervous. Would I be inspired and ready to complete my work in each book within the time frame? Would the muse be around for all of them?

When the books started rolling in, I would open the packages ceremoniously, steeping a pot of tea and clearing out space on my art table. I would pull out the paper bits I had saved for particular books and listen to what the book was saying to me. Each journal truly emanated the spirit and style of the artist who made it, and at first it was quite a challenge to hold strong to my own vision and what I conceived to be my personal style. Working with the spirit of collaboration, I eased myself into the mingling of visions and images, getting my feet wet at first, then diving right into what turned out to be a very animated conversation of colors. I would listen closely to hear what the book was saying to me and do my best as an interpreter.

—Karen Michel

Violet & Green

WE THINK VERY LITTLE OF TIME
HASTEN IT ONWARD. WE RECA
THIS WANDER THROUGH THE
OUR OWN. PASCAL

Violet & Green

WE ANTICIPATE THE FUTURE AS BEING TOO SLOW, AND WITH A VIEW TO
... TO STAY IT AS TOO SWIFTLY GONE. WE ARE SO THOUGHTLESS THAT WE
... THEM ARE NOT HERE, REGARDLESS ONLY OF THE MOMENT THAT IS ACTUALLY

Violet & Green was a set of colors I was wild about. I knew right away I wanted to use a stereo view of a little girl in a lily conservatory, but my actual stereo view card was bent; it was no good trying to use the original in a flat format. Instead I made a collage and transferred it onto a gorgeous piece of white fabric I had from Nina. I stitched some lovely green borders on the fabric and mounted it all onto an amazing piece of violet-colored Japanese paper. Perfect!

—Sarah Fishburn

Artist: Claudine Hellmuth

*K*aren's Violet & Green journal was such fun! I love the way she used staples in her artwork; I would never think to use staples that way. For her journal, I wanted to do something a little whimsical. I used part of an old sketchbook page I had created, color-copied it and glued it down. Then I painted and collaged over it. I added little stick-on stars because I think they are fun and kitschy. I also created a small collage in a hanging papier-mâché frame. I glued purple buttons to the frame in keeping with the theme of the book.

—Claudine Hellmuth

I loved Violet &Green. I coveted this journal because the color combination was so satisfying (it was with regret that I sent it on). The circle punch was brand new to me so I had to play with it. Karen has a penchant for color and symbolism from India. She often put incense in a pocket on someone's page, and although I wanted to do something Indian in motif, I decided to continue with the faces and added pockets for holding little quotes. The tags are circles glued on tiny gold tags from Lynne. The circle stamp is my own carved stamp, and I use it a lot. The dots are stamped through sequin scrim.

—Linn C. Jacobs

Artist: Linn C. Jacobs

Violet & Green

Karen sent me her journal to complete after it made its rounds to everyone else. She wanted very much for me to make my entry, because we had become good friends while teaching at various workshops across the country and felt a common thread above and beyond simple teaching and artwork. I feel that this was my finest entry, perhaps because it was the final one, and because it is a combination of both paper art and jewelry. Why the combination? I wanted her to have something special from my heart. She is a special person, with the kindest of hearts, and it was very important that I share that feeling with others. Her pages, too, have a story of a gypsy—a magician named Applesauce.

For Karen's necklace, I pulled treasures from my own private stash—river shards of pottery, faceted freshwater pearls, vintage beads. At the necklace's base is a frame of brass holding a number of "cards"—tiny images and words collaged and sandwiched in between sheets of mica and fastened together with minute eyelets, then stacked and held within the frame. The cards can be taken out and read individually, then arranged in any order for placement back within the necklace piece. It represents the story as written on the journal's pages, and within an envelope attached between the paper. I also attached large sheets of mica to the paper pages themselves, mirroring the necklace and tying together the central story for my friend, who loves a magician.

—Nina Bagley

Always in our

dreams

Who is she, you ask?
I'm surprised that you do not recognize
her loving face,
for she is the angel
of your beautiful green and purple dreams
She spends every night setting up hopes
for the next day's softness...
making sure that you will hear
the call of the wren,
the lowing of the cattle in the glen.
If there is rain,
she promises prisms of light

Violet & Green

drops Grace

s are heavy,

ose dreams

your sighs

pers

f courage

recall

to fade away

left

a day

Talismans for a magnificent woman
who favors the colors of
gardeners and kings, and
whose lover is
a beautiful magician; one who
speaks liltingly of applesauce
(this can always be tinted
with sweet wines
and berries)

Within is a
tale
of the

loveliest shades

of

fairydust

on

roses that bloom

at the

mention of your name

Artist: Nina Bagley

For Karen's journal, I made two fabric panels separated by a page that I painted with watercolors, adding a line from one of the songs in the movie Moulin Rouge: "One day I'll fly away." This gave me the flying theme, so I printed dominoes and wings on fabric and sewed the little flying people together. I then added buttons and fibers to the fabric collage.

—Keely Barham

Violet & Green

The pages I did in the Violet & Green book reflected what I was doing in my studio at the time. I am interested in repeat patterns, but here I considered motifs and patterns that stand on their own. They are done in many layers on canvas using stamps and stencils. One thing I like about art journals is that they contain techniques that are "stopped," and my entry is an example of this. I no longer work like this; the technique has evolved. But it is interesting to see what I was doing then and I think I might go back and try this some more. Violet & Green was an interesting color scheme that I had never worked with before. Very sophisticated.

—*Anne Bagby*

Violet & Green

Karen's colorful little book insisted I be playful with my entry. I began painting in violet, green and turquoise, then stamped some flowers for a retro style. I had to use the Partridge Family theme song "C'mon Get Happy" as a mini-CD enclosure. I pulled a denim pocket from my son's old jeans and tucked in a packet of Pop Rocks, a candy I remember from the '70s. A greeting card with two little girls dressed in green and purple coats was a perfect little insert; I had them claim to be from the David Cassidy fan club, just as I had been.

—Michelle Ward

Monica Riffe's Green journal reflects the artist's sense of fun and whimsy. Monica constructed her journal by painting the cover of an old library book and embellishing it with actual paintbrushes. She wired pages from a store-bought journal lengthwise inside the cover so the artists could work in a compact, vertical space.

Monica's childlike spirit proved infectious; the artists responded to her Green journal with a bit of whimsy of their own. Nina Bagley tore out pages from a vintage children's storybook and created a kind of secret garden out of barkcloth. Marylinn Kelly paid homage to Hoot, the Girl Scout leader who was a "positive force" in her youth.

To the artists, green meant climbing trees (Nina), marveling at the many shades of green to be found in their own backyards (Lynne Perrella), and relaxing in a garden, dreaming up characters like "The Pine Tree Nun" (Sarah Fishburn). The journal left many with a newfound appreciation of green in its many shades and variations.

"Surely Monica dreams of green?" Nina writes. "I know I do now."

FIELD GUIDE
1 2

True Colors-GR...

green is
girl scouts

VeRde

Green

PEA

listen

Sweet peas and seedlings.
The unfurling of tender leaves,
the return of green grass
on the hillsides in springtime.
A journal to celebrate new growth.

ORIGINATING ARTIST:
Monica Riffe

When I grabbed green as the color for my journal, I must admit I was thinking my choices were limited to the traditional rainbow. Within that spectrum of colors, I felt green had the most variation. There was sea foam, olive, emerald, lime, and sage. As the color choices came pouring in, it became apparent that the other artists were thinking "outside the box." They had selected white, black, metallic, and a combination of colors: pink and orange, blue and ochre, green and violet! I am glad I chose the color I did, though, because the journal seemed to leap into being without much effort or artistic struggle.
***
I get my inspiration from whatever is cluttering my studio. When we began this project, I had an old book that had been given to me to alter called *The ABC of Color.* This was a perfect choice. Its cover became my Green journal cover, which I altered with paints and inlaid with various green crayon wrappers. I ripped out its innards, and they found their way into many of the *True Colors* journals. Those collaged bits acted as artistic prompts and spiritual links between the journals.

By happenstance, the pages from a purchased Canson journal fit perfectly into my *ABC of Color* book. Using the holes that were already in the black Canson papers, I drilled matching holes in the covers of *The ABC of Color,* and bound them with coiled wire. Maybe the vertical format wasn't ideal, because after all of the artists worked on the journal, it was so full it couldn't close. If I had known it would be so bulky in its finished state, I might have bound the pages into the spine of the book. I pasted a postcard of Shirley Ende-Saxe's into my Green journal, because it was green, and Shirley and I are mail art chums.

In another bit of serendipity, *The ABC of Color* had a library card on the inside back cover that had exactly 15 empty slots for the 15 artists' signatures. It makes me happy to think that *The ABC of Color,* which was never checked out when it sat on a library shelf, came to life as an altered book in the *True Colors* project.
***
True (color) confessions: At times, I fretted over what I was going to do in a certain book. What I learned over the course of this project was that if I just started working, the art would flow. In other words, I learned to trust my muse. That was the gem of this journey for me.

—Monica Riffe

I worked on Forest Floor and Monica's Green book simultaneously and had a terrible time with both of them. I spent a long time on the sewing, and was disappointed with the results. (When working on such a tight schedule, there is little time for a redo). I also didn't think the size of the books and the color worked well with my initial resolve to use the figure on each page. It seemed like green connotes nature instead. So the figures ended up as bugs, frogs and lizards, which I love because they have such wonderful shapes.

—Anne Bagby

Green

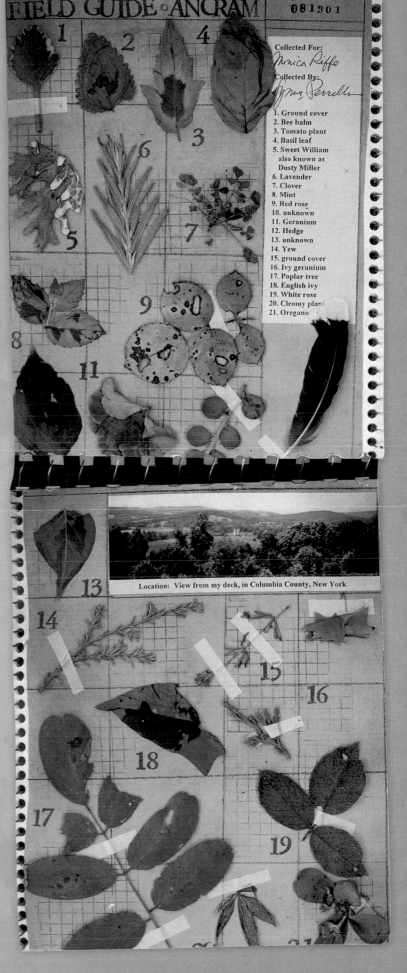

FIELD GUIDE • ANCRAM   081301

Collected For:
Monica Riffe
Collected By:
Lynne Perrella

1. Ground cover
2. Bee balm
3. Tomato plant
4. Basil leaf
5. Sweet William
   also known as
   Dusty Miller
6. Lavender
7. Clover
8. Mint
9. Red rose
10. unknown
11. Geranium
12. Hedge
13. unknown
14. Yew
15. ground cover
16. Ivy geranium
17. Poplar tree
18. English ivy
19. White rose
20. Cleomy plant
21. Oregano

Location: View from my deck, in Columbia County, New York

Monica's book arrived at the height of summer, in mid-August. I looked through the pages, looked outside my door and realized, "Everything I need is right here" (as is frequently the case in art). I started walking around our land, looking with renewed appreciation at the zillion shades of green. I pinched leaves and pulled sprigs, keeping the little cuttings in my apron pocket. Doing this page for Monica started me on a new habit of pasting natural things onto my own journal pages. By making color prints of the pages, we "save" the leaves and other flotsam and jetsam that will eventually crumble and fall away. Now we have a memory of how it felt to select those elements, maybe even remembering the lingering smell of lavender or the pungent aroma of a yew branch. I included the photo taken from my deck as evidence of the many shades of green in Ancram, hoping that it would entice Monica to come and take a look someday.

—Lynne Perrella

Artist: Lisa Renner

I started with a background of copper cardstock that I covered in a soft green patina using metal surfacing products by Modern Options. I painted fabric with acrylic paints and sewed a pouch, stitching beads on the sides. I applied a rust finish to a piece of chipboard with the same surfacing products and cut it into a tag shape. The embellishment on the tag is made from polymer clay that was rubbed with chalks and stamped with rubber stamps in Crafters Ink. The tag nests inside the pouch, which sports a fiber tassel.

—Lisa Renner

Monica's Green journal is the size of a girl's diary, and that may have helped bring up the thought of Girl Scouts. For me, green is Girl Scouts; I was actively involved through the 12th grade and wanted to tell a story about the woman who had been our leader and stayed our friend. Her scout camp name was Hoot and I created a paper owl shape with folded wings to hold her story. The other page used pieces from a book on Girl Scout uniforms through the years, showing badges and a paper doll with outfits. Monica's journal gave me a chance to honor Hoot and the positive force she was in my life.

—Marylinn Kelly

Artist: Marylinn Kelly

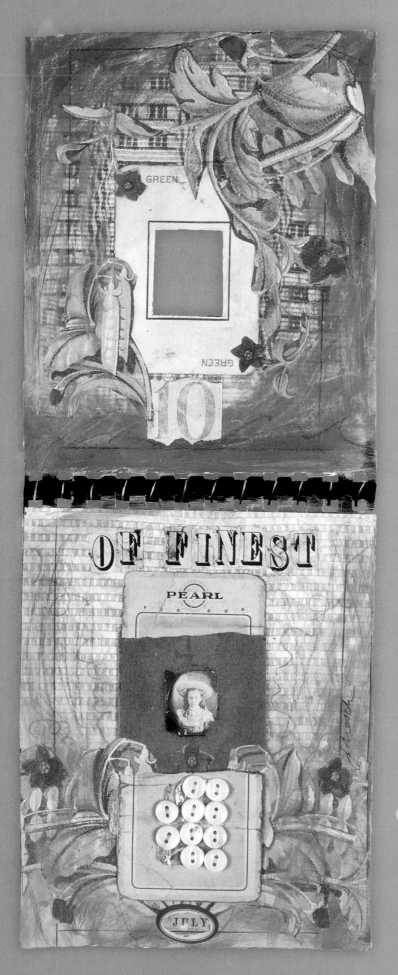

Green

Another smaller-size offering, Monica's amusing and clever Green journal brought the words "sweet pea" to mind right away. I knew just where to find a decorative border of these dainty heirloom flowers. They surround an old playing card with the word "green," cut open to reveal a teeny photo of a girl in her straw bonnet. I placed her between a torn button card with mother-of-pearl buttons lined up like peas in a pod. I couldn't help putting additional buttons inside the pods. Old cardboard anagram tiles and cut-out letters help spell out "Sweet Pea … of finest pearl."

—Judi Riesch

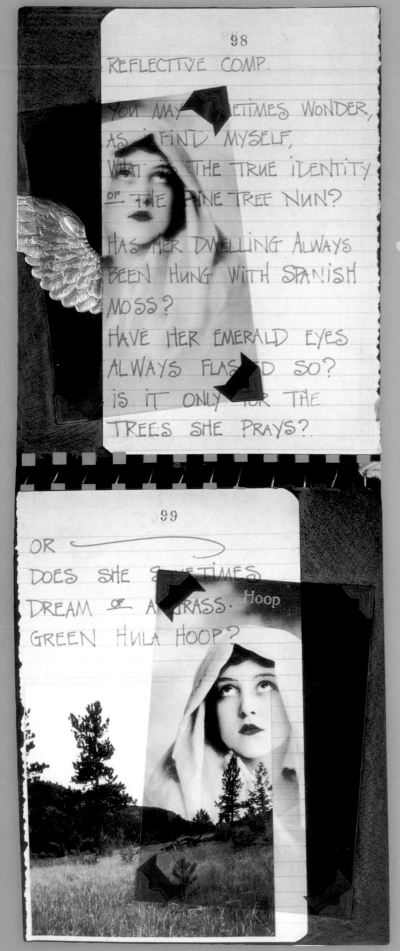

98

REFLECTIVE COMP.

YOU MAY SOMETIMES WONDER,
AS I FIND MYSELF,
WHAT IS THE TRUE IDENTITY
OF THE PINE TREE NUN?

HAS HER DWELLING ALWAYS
BEEN HUNG WITH SPANISH
MOSS?

HAVE HER EMERALD EYES
ALWAYS FLASHED SO?
IS IT ONLY FOR THE
TREES SHE PRAYS?

99

OR
DOES SHE SOMETIMES
DREAM OF A GRASS. Hoop
GREEN HULA HOOP?

Artist: Sarah Fishburn

Woo-hoo! Another small book. With Monica, I knew it was OK to go all out with the humor aspect. When we get together, we can hardly contain ourselves for laughing over one thing or another. Her son Evan helped me come up with the concept of "The Pine Tree Nun" one morning as we sat in Monica's backyard. I imagined the nun writing a composition. It was fun to make the extra little hanging piece from a coaster, already green with peas.

—Sarah Fishburn

Because Monica always makes me laugh, or at least smile while reading her e-mails, I wanted to do something funny in her journal. My big mistake was to use my new glossy golden gel medium on both pages—which wasn't so funny. Monica later told me they stuck together. I have since discontinued the use of gel medium on the inside of my journals. It was an experiment I should have tried before doing it someone else's journal.

—Teesha Moore

Artist: Claudine Hellmuth

I created my page in Monica's journal using an image of a statue and these little sparkly beads I had become obsessed with. I was using them everywhere! I liked making little halos with them. This piece was simple; it still feels unfinished to me, and I wish I could work on it again. I keep reminding myself that this project was about experimentation and process, not the finished product!

—Claudine Hellmuth

Bad Idea #101
Keeping your Glue Stick and lip balm in the Same pocket.

teesha '01

Artist: Teesha Moore

This one was easy. Monica has a childlike spirit, full of whimsy and appreciation for all things fun and amazing. "Aha," I thought. The garden. I came across more of my beloved barkcloth for her page, using a predominantly green scrap, and attached a wire garden gate with letter charms from my jewelry designs that spell out "g-r-e-e-n." Then I added a bronze key, metal vines and wire twisted for more vines—simple! Rather than gluing the fabric down, I attached it at the top with vintage mother-of-pearl buttons that had been dyed green, allowing the viewer to lift the fabric and see what secrets are behind the gate. I had saved a catalog photo of an open-door green wardrobe, and the notion of a secret one in Monica's book spoke immediately to me of the world of Narnia. Inside is a woman with an umbrella, and behind her I dotted small flakes of gold snow. Extending the childlike theme, I placed a page taken from a child's vintage storybook of a young girl and boy sitting up in a tree, branches full of green leaves all around them. Below, in pencil childlike scrawl, I wrote the words, "Sometimes my brother and I stay up in the tree and dream of green." Surely Monica dreams of green? I know I do now.

—Nina Bagley

Green

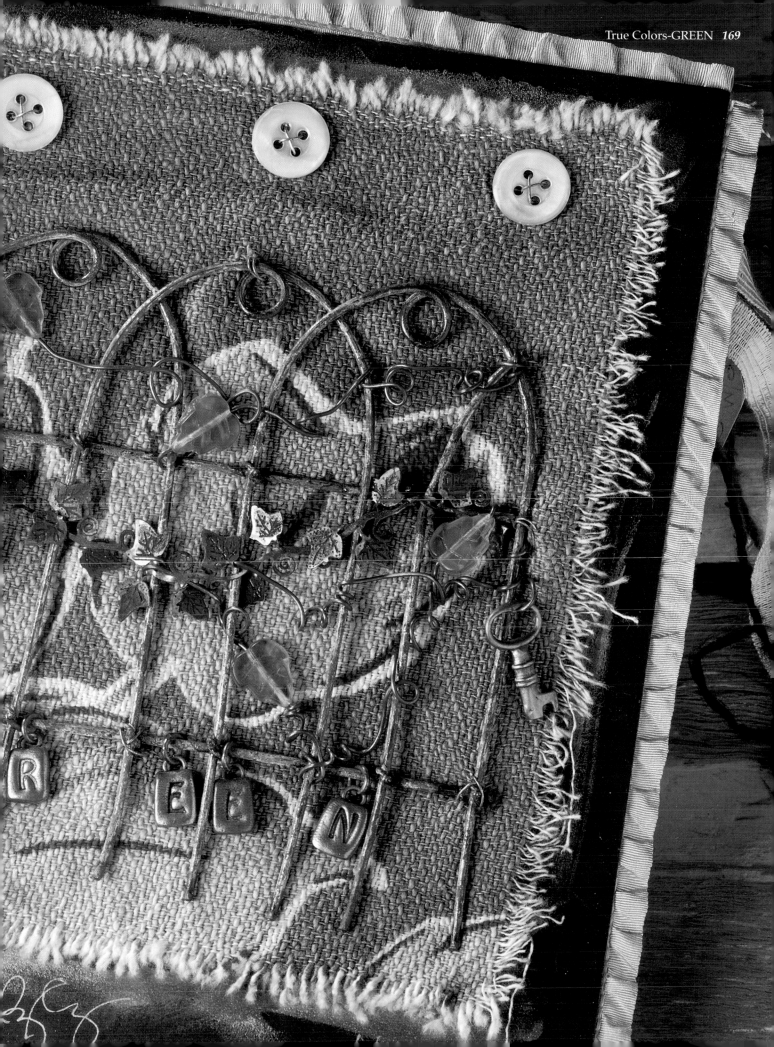

Lisa Hoffman, lover of nature and defender of trees, chose not a color but a concept for the first of her two journals, Forest Floor. Lisa wanted the cover of her book to feel like a portal to a magical, woodsy place. Adorned with fibers and a twig (a trademark feature of Lisa's pages), the metal-plated cover does indeed feel like a door to another, exotic world.

Forest Floor is one of the more tactile journals of the project. Many of the artists followed Lisa's lead and added fibers, fabric, beads, buttons, ribbons and other touchable elements to their pages. With a palette inspired by nature, they pulled in images of birds' nests, leafy glades, frogs, Druids, woodland waifs, and homey refuges from the elements. As an homage to Lisa, a couple of the artists (Nina Bagley and Lisa Renner) even stitched twigs onto their entries.

More than just a physical place, Forest Floor represents that hidden refuge you go to in your mind when the world is still, and all you can hear is the rustle of pine needles beneath your feet.

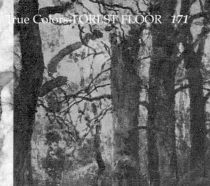

Forest Floor

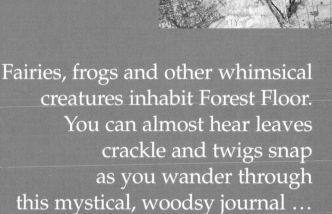

Fairies, frogs and other whimsical
creatures inhabit Forest Floor.
You can almost hear leaves
crackle and twigs snap
as you wander through
this mystical, woodsy journal …

FOREST
FLOOR

ENTRYWAY - - - - -

ORIGINATING ARTIST:
Lisa Hoffman

I was one of the latecomers to the project, due to a studio move and a disconnected computer. Thanks to a mutual friend, I heard that Lynne was looking for me. When we finally connected and she described the concept, my first comment was: "Sounds like the basic colors are covered." She then explained that the color ways were variable, like Sunset and Autumn, at which point I replied, "O.K., so we could go pretty esoteric, like Forest Floor?" I was joking, but Lynne started this amazing stream-of-consciousness description of the things that entered her mind when she heard the words Forest Floor. Suddenly, I could "see" the cover in my mind's eye. We had a winner!

***

The serendipitous part of the story is that the tree theme has always been significant in my work and in my family script. As a political activist, my great-grandmother was responsible for the official Mothers' Day tree on the White House grounds. She had trees planted to commemorate the mothers of American presidents. A generation later, my mother took up the mantel and became a tree hugger in the truest sense of the word. When a line of bulldozers moved in to remove a beautiful and ancient stand of

willows behind our home in suburban D.C., she stood in front of them with the conviction of a Green Peace warrior. She lost that battle, and I was given a very early dose of reality when the landscape around me went from green, lush and beautiful to a cold and dirty slab of concrete. Where were my trees?

***

You will often see wrapped twigs in my work, as well as pieces and parts of anything woody, which brings me to the cover art of my journal. I grabbed a blank photo album that featured a silver metallic cover-piece in the spirit of King Arthur and the Knights of the Round Table. The center insert came with a postcard, which I removed and replaced with my own work. I wanted the cover to invite the reader to touch, so I had to integrate something soft. I used ribbon, twine and various threads to stand up and beckon. I kept the palette earthy and warm. I used rubber stamp alphabets and worked in a loose fashion to create a subtle suggestion of whimsy. The cover implies a doorway or portal into the realm of possibility. I wanted the True Colorists, as well as the reader, to be seduced!

—Lisa Hoffman

BRAINS & HUMOR
WILL OPEN ANY
DOOR ...

EVA CHASE

FOREST
FLOOR
ENTRYWAY - - - - -

SPIRIT OF THE WOODS

Forest Floor

I worked on this just after September 11, 2001. That was a stunned, frozen time for all of us; I felt incapable of creating artwork. How futile! How shallow a motion, in a time of such deep grieving. Yet, as I picked up paper, brush and glue, some of the sorrow began to ebb, though temporarily, and I was able to at least express my own aching sadness for a country whose losses were unfathomable. Here in Lisa's pages is a lovely poem by my own North Carolina's Fred Chappell, printed on vintage bookpaper and floating freely between clear acetate. These were sacred words for the grief we all felt and continue to feel, with the words, "let us linger, as we may, within the grove" underlined as a nod to Lisa's choice of the Forest Floor color. As an accompaniment to this simple but very strong page, I constructed another design using vintage floral barkcloth, very knobby and woods-like in texture, as a background, leaving the frayed edges alone with their wonderful trailing string because they reminded me of vines along a forest floor. At the pages' edge, I fastened a pencil fashioned from a rhododendron stick, and upon its base I stamped the words "into the grove." I then attached several of my own jewelry castings—acorns and birds—to fill out the forest atmosphere. Can you hear the birds singing to the little spirit of the woods?

—Nina Bagley

How Lisa Hoffman had time to create not one but two
remarkable journals is beyond me! I had a great time working
in both journals. For Forest Floor, I used some old Xerox
copies I had, painted and collaged over them, then went back
in with oil pastel. I scratched off the pastel to create texture
and drew back into it with pencil.

—Claudine Hellmuth

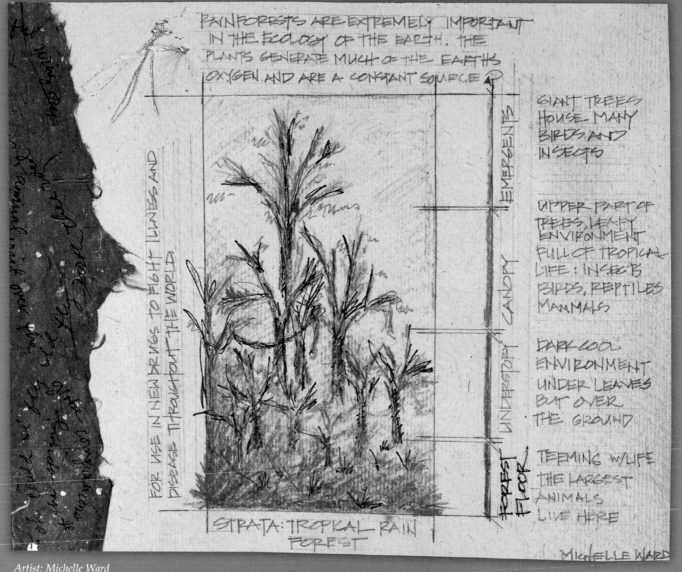

RAINFORESTS ARE EXTREMELY IMPORTANT IN THE ECOLOGY OF THE EARTH. THE PLANTS GENERATE MUCH OF THE EARTHS OXYGEN AND ARE A CONSTANT SOURCE

FOR USE IN NEW DRUGS TO FIGHT ILLNESS AND DISEASE THROUGHOUT THE WORLD

EMERGENTS

GIANT TREES HOUSE MANY BIRDS AND INSECTS

CANOPY

UPPER PART OF TREES, LEAFY ENVIRONMENT FULL OF TROPICAL LIFE: INSECTS BIRDS, REPTILES MAMMALS

UNDERSTORY

DARK COOL ENVIRONMENT UNDER LEAVES BUT OVER THE GROUND

FOREST FLOOR

TEEMING W/LIFE THE LARGEST ANIMALS LIVE HERE

STRATA: TROPICAL RAIN FOREST

MICHELLE WARD

Artist: Michelle Ward

I hit my stride working on Lisa's Forest Floor journal. I did my pages as well as the front and back inside covers. I incorporated many fun materials, such as antiquated library cards, a tin bird sitting on a wire branch and a vintage book cover titled The New Forest, *which my sister found in England.*

—Monica Riffe

Artist: Monica Riffe

rain has
splash
plant has
shell a

when i was 8 my
father took us to
the forest behind
our house to hunt

rain has showered far her drip
splash and trickle running
plant has flowered in the sand
shell and pebble sunning

so begins another spring
green leaves and of berries
chiff-chaff eggs are painted by
motherbird eating cherries

in a misty tangled sky
fast a wind is blowing
in a newborn rabbit's heart
river life is flowing

so begins another spring
green leaves and of berries
chiff-chaff eggs are painted by
motherbird eating cherries

from the dark and whetted soil
petals are unfolding
from the stony village kirk
easter bells of old ring

so begins another spring
green leaves and of berries
chiff-chaff eggs are painted by
motherbird eating cherries

faeries's debris!

ribbon.

for fossils. som
we found other things.
rocks and bits of

PINE • Long Life, Family Love—needles radiating
from a common centre.

Forest Floor

...en i was 8 my mother gave me a book that...

...early begins with the following words:

...his is the forest primeval. The murmuring

...pines and the hemlocks,

Bearded with moss, and in garments green,

indistinct in the twilight,

REPUBLIQUE CENTRA... REPUBLIQUE CENTRA...

DEAREST... WE HA... ...DED TO REMAIN... HERE AMONG THE TREES. PLEASE JOIN US WHEN YOU CAN?

Stand like Druids of eld.

Forest Floor was the first book I had to work on after I
finished my own pages in the Red journal. The magical title
made me think of a fairyland, and the pages I did in it
reflect a slightly fractured forest scene the way I imagined
it, as seen through the eyes of a fairy child.

—Sarah Fishburn

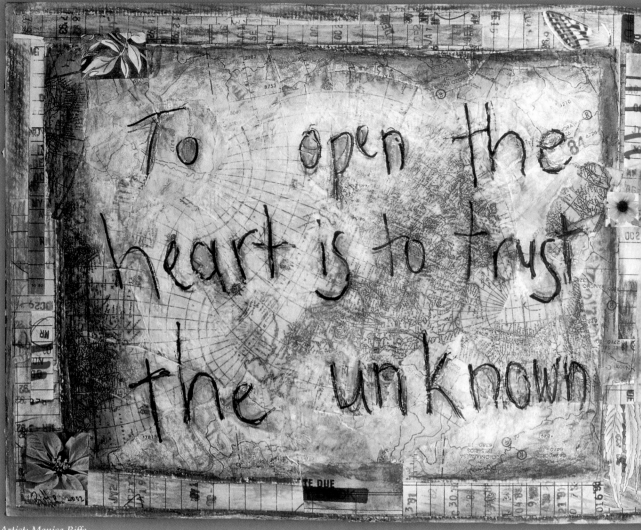

Artist: Monica Riffe

Forest Floor, by name alone, evokes an earthy, woodsy atmosphere. I couldn't wait to breathe it in! It arrived here in November, when the fall colors were in full swing. I planned my pages, knowing I wanted to use beautiful bird's nest paper I had tucked away, awaiting a perfect opportunity. The Bradford Pear trees in my front yard graced themselves with what appeared to be a bouquet of leaves ranging in color from fiery red to golden yellow to speckled green edged in amber. I plucked what I needed and dried them in Microfleur (US ArtQuest). Because they are brittle, I carefully glued each leaf to a piece of cardstock for support and cut them all out. The reinforced leaves were then glued to the bird's nest paper and covered with a mesh pocket made from window screen sprayed with gold paint. I placed additional leaves on my color copier and copied them onto vellum. I then staggered torn vellum pages and sewed them together to make a booklet. I edged the booklet with beautiful hand-dyed ribbon. The poem was written for this page.

—Lisa Renner

She leaps across the forest floor
and smiles when no one sees;
With visions old
and eyes twinkling gold
she dreams among the leaves.

Lisa Renner

Artist: Lisa Renner

Forest Floor

Along thy wild and willowed shore,
The fairies played on the Forest Floor.

THE WEEPING AND THE PUSSY WILLOW

willow

FILE: FOREST FAIRY

FILE: FOREST FLOOR

Fairy elves,
whose midnight revels
by a forest side
or fountain,
some belated
peasant sees,
or dreams he sees,
while overhead
the moon
sits arbitress.

John Milton

ARBITRESS *from arbiter, arbitrator*

ar·bi·ter (är′b-tr) *n.* 1. One chosen or appoint-
ed to judge or decide a disputed issue; an arbitrator. 2.
One who has the power to judge or ordain at will:
an arbiter of fashion. See Synonyms at *judge.*

Lisa's introduction to the Forest Floor, with her account of her
great-grandmother's concern for the environment, set a
meaningful tone to her color choice. I began with a spread paying
homage to rain forests with a drawing of the hierarchy of forest
contents. Then, after a sighting of fireflies on a summer evening,
I included a journal entry about forest fairies. I altered a found
poem: "Along thy wild and willowed shore, the fairies played on
the forest floor." This allowed me to include a favorite Cicely
Mary Barker image, the Willow Fairy.

—*Michelle Ward*

Illustration of *The Willow Fairy*
Copyright © The Estate of Cicely Mary Barker, 1940, 1990

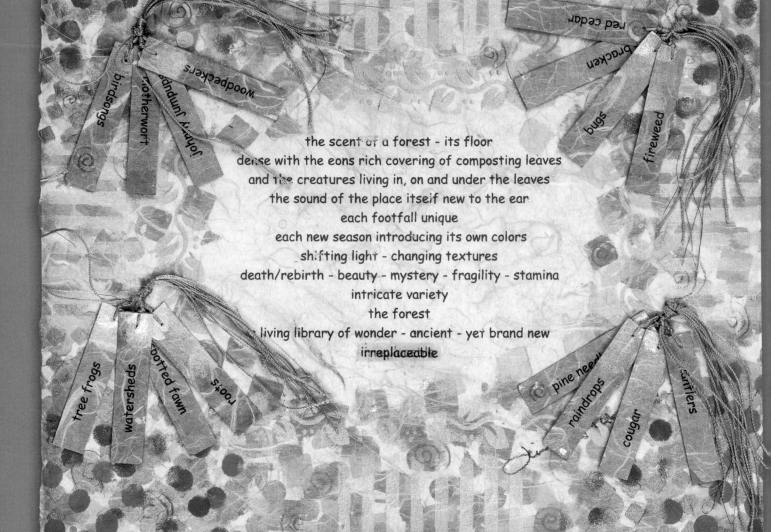

the scent of a forest - its floor
dense with the eons rich covering of composting leaves
and the creatures living in, on and under the leaves
the sound of the place itself new to the ear
each footfall unique
each new season introducing its own colors
shifting light - changing textures
death/rebirth - beauty - mystery - fragility - stamina
intricate variety
the forest
living library of wonder - ancient - yet brand new
irreplaceable

Artist: Linn C. Jacobs

This was the last journal I worked in, and I never had the actual journal in my hands. Lisa Hoffman e-mailed me a picture of what the cover looked like, and I knew the size so I went from there. Time was of the essence, as it was late in the game (May 2002). I thought about the actual forest floor and wrote a little piece about it. I found a quote out of Rachel Carson's book, The Sense of Wonder, and printed the words on gauzy thin paper, stenciling around the edges with some simple square motifs. My piece needed something more, so that's how the tags came to be used with more woodsy, earthy words. Just as I was putting the pages into the envelope to mail—yikes—I spotted a spelling error. I had barely any thin paper left and little time, but I fixed it. I hope it's the only one.

—Linn C. Jacobs

Forest Floor was a real challenge for me. The previous entries all seemed so perfect for this journal's environmental theme that at first I could not find my own direction. While searching for inspiration, I discovered a quote about the woods in winter. It described old gray leaves that grow to look like lace, and I remembered saving some of these very leaves the winter before. I fashioned specimen envelopes to house these findings, then created a spread to suggest a forest floor during this season. Using snowy vellum, paint, doilies, and feathers, I tried to capture the gray and cold environment. Two studio photographs of the same woman dressed in her winter finery, muff and all, keep company with the quiet, shadowy forest.

—Judi Riesch

Forest Floor

Artist: Judi Riesch

Claudine Hellmuth's Green journal was a favorite of the artists. They loved its compact size and well-worn pages. Upon receiving it, Lynne Perrella sent out an e-mail to the group saying, "I have Claudine's journal in hand. Literally! It fits right into my hand. What a dear book. On this sizzling summer day, this is a little safe zone of cool, calm green."

Claudine chose a vintage photo album for her journal with a beautiful, tattered leather cover. In the center, where an old tintype used to be, she created one of her charming minimalist portraits. She placed a tiny girl in a First Holy Communion dress against—what else?—a solid green painted background.

For their part, the artists applied layer upon layer of green, making the most of the album's small (4¼"x5½") pages. In this journal, green is the color of money. Four-leaf clovers. Faux postage from Ireland. Antique ribbon. Some entries, like Lisa Renner's abstract collage of paper and metal, were a half-dozen layers deep.

Claudine's little Green journal proves the old saying: Good things come in small packages.

ev-er green

[vairday]

Green

A bridal bouquet
with mint green flowers.
A kelly green moon.
An emerald waterfall.
See the world through
green-colored glasses …

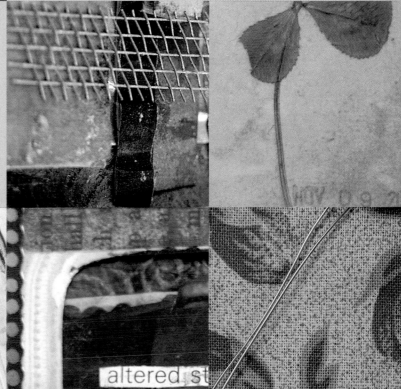

altered st

ORIGINATING ARTIST:
Claudine Hellmuth

When Lynne first asked me to be a part of this project, I had a difficult time picking a color. Everyone else seemed to be picking beautiful colors, and I was stumped. Finally I resorted to picking from a pile of paint chips with my eyes closed. The fates guided me to green, and I went with it.

I knew I wanted to work small in my journal. I like tiny books; they feel so intimate and special. On a practical level, I knew that having a smaller book would keep shipping costs down, and it wouldn't take as long for each artist to work in the journal.

I had an old tintype album sitting in my studio. It was worn and old and looked like it could use some love. I thought the tintype frames would make nice pages, and each artist could work inside the frames. I patched up the book with masking tape and string and began working on the front cover design. The leatherwork on the cover was already very lovely, so I didn't want to cover it completely. Instead I worked in the oval shape in the middle of the cover, painted it green and added an image of a girl in her Communion dress. To the front of her dress, I pasted on the phonetic spelling of green (verde) in Italian. As a final step, I tied the whole book with a natural string and added a tag. Perfect!
***

When I first started working on the other journals, I was so nervous; I didn't want to mess up anyone's book. I would create a separate entry for the journal, then adhere my work to the page. It took awhile for me to feel free enough to really work in each artist's book. Once I crossed that hurdle, I started enjoying the process. I tried to make myself try new things in the pages that I wasn't doing in my "regular" artwork.

I started experimenting with drawing in my collages, like in the Blue & Ochre journal. I wanted to try new things and use these journals as a format for experimentation. Once I got past the fear of "ruining" a book and began to experiment, I started to have a good time. I gave myself a time limit for each journal so that I wouldn't get overwhelmed thinking I had to make a masterpiece in each one.

I gave myself 1½ hours for each journal. Sometimes, if you force yourself to work fast, you can stomp out the inner critic. Because you are working too fast to be judging your work, as you go along you can sometimes make breakthroughs. You might not love the work, but you will find hints of breakthroughs in it—elements and ways of working that you wouldn't have normally tried if you let your inner critic have time to speak up. For this journal exchange, I wanted to make myself get past the product and really focus on the process of creating.

—Claudine Hellmuth

When Claudine's ancient little book arrived, I wrote to her that I felt I'd been invited to plan a party in a ruin. Pages were falling out, and that simply added to the charm. Because I love to draw green crescent moons, that's what I chose to draw for inside the frame. The moon made me think of bodies that reflect light rather than generate it (we can't ALL be suns). So I added some words to that effect over a painted and stamped background, along with a tiny sun that was smaller, for once, than the mirrored moon.

—Marylinn Kelly

For some, the task is to generate light, for others, to reflect it.

Artist: Marylinn Kelly

Artist: Keely Barham

I knew exactly what I would contribute to Claudine's journal when I saw its petite size and the shape of the pages. I had just learned to do seed bead embroidery, so I traced the opening in the page onto ultrasuede. I then embroidered a sun setting over a green field with seed beads and bugle beads, using a bone face bead for the sun. I covered the page with a green leaf patterned fabric and trimmed it with satin ribbon.

—Keely Barham

Green

Claudine's Green journal was the very first journal I worked in, and my studio was the first stop for the little album itself. I began by thinking about how to portray the West and the natural world in a wee bit of space. I used a color copy of a book cover about the same age as the album. I think it is American Notes by Rudyard Kipling. For imagery, I chose Coyote the Trickster, a common figure in American Southwest literature . He could be a guardian for the little book as it made its way around the country. I added a little tag-like piece of polymer clay for embellishment with my favorite leaf stamp.

—Linn C. Jacobs

There was one empty page following my journal entry, opposite Sarah's page. It was asking to be covered! I wanted it to complement Sarah's existing page, so I followed her lead and incorporated a transparency. I selected a botanical tapestry filled with rich, earthy colors, and printed it onto acetate. Under the transparency is sage vellum with a center cutout that allows one to get the actual color view of the tapestry. The two layers were attached with sage eyelets over brass washers, then glued onto the page. For a final touch, I added an old dictionary definition of green.

—Michelle Ward

When I took Claudine's class, she tried to get me to quit my work sooner, to leave things off and do a little less. So I had a great idea to make a very simple, perfect little picture that would symbolize Claudine and her work. Since she was getting married, I decided to use a vintage photograph of a bride. Well, I could not keep it simple. It positively screamed, "More! More!" So I did it—I added more and more. I think it turned out the busiest of all the work I did. I wish I could go back and try again. I know I can do a simple picture. But this is definitely not it. I am sure she looked at the page and said, "That one has got to be Anne's."

—Anne Bagby

Claudine's book was known as "The Thumbelina Book," and it truly deserved a special name of its own. It arrived in a small, nearly weightless box, and I could swear I heard a fairyland orchestra playing a lilting waltz as I took my first look through it. The small openings (used for framing and displaying long-ago portraits) seemed like they were ready for a new assignment. I decided the humble dollar bill, with all of its detailed engraving, would be a perfect example of green. I pulled out a whole stash of different rubber stamps, plus every green inkpad I had, and began covering the old ivory photo frames with stampings. The final touch was an old circle template that I had since art school. Its murky green color had great potential, and the nostalgic significance of it made me want to "save" it in some way. A simple mundane studio tool that I had used for more than 30 years and had tossed away without much thought—suddenly it seemed worthy of being rescued and worthy of keeping, because of the quiet lessons of the little Green journal.

—Lynne Perrella

Artist: Judi Riesch

This diminutive Green journal is such a dear object. Opening this teeny treasure was a real treat. I enjoyed seeing what each artist decided to slip into the frames. The familiar format gave way to quick ideas, and before I knew it, I was tucking an old stencil with the letter G, for Green of course, into the photograph opening. The cabinet card frame pages were perfect for edging with antique ribbons and a selection of buttons. Maps from a discarded travel book, a tintype and a transparency finish the entry. My pages were somewhat fragile to start with and needed a little TLC, but with a bit of tape and paint they were on the mend—ageless and evergreen.

—Judi Riesch

Claudine's little green lady required a switch of creative gears because of its diminutive size. I pulled out all of my green papers and decided to make a small 3-D collage. I assembled it from snippets of gold, copper, bits of wire, mesh, and window screen. Acrylic paint was used as the border, accented with gold Krylon pen.

—Lisa Renner

Artist: Lisa Renner

Green

The "Anglo Maiden" layout was born out of my need to call attention to a very odd concept. I had recently run across this entire book of vintage, well-executed and slightly sexy Indian Maiden images. The fact that they all looked like white girls with Indian clothes simply had to be addressed. In a book so lovely and tiny, my only chance was to convey my message in the title. I scanned the image, placing it inside the page's center cutout, originally intended for photos. I needed to incorporate the forest-y and natural theme that the image's background featured, so I used various greens and a portion of a huge pine bough rubber stamp. A real seedpod served as the top focal point. I decided to toss in a few pieces of painted and dyed muslin for a bit more dimension and texture. I actually love this image, but I couldn't let the irony and subtle message slip by unnoticed.

—Lisa Hoffman

This tiny treasure was a surprising treat, a lesson in scale, minimalism and structure. With the cabinet card openings as a starting point, I inserted simple yet personal representations of green. The faux postage from Ireland represents my heritage. I included the four leaf clover because I have incredible luck finding handfuls each summer.

—*Michelle Ward*

Lisa Hoffman created the Aqua journal after Forest Floor was mistakenly presumed to be lost. She wanted a journal that was different in style from the others, one that was small and "sassy." She brazenly called her journal Aqua Exotica, and adorned it with roses and a geisha to contrast with her sky blue color.

For the artists, the summery Aqua journal was fun, light—a party that traveled by parcel post. In Lynne Perrella's words, the journal "was small and chunky and playful, almost like a teenage diary." The artists filled the small spiral-bound journal with images of flowers, seashells, stars, birds, butterflies, geishas, and girls. Aqua is home to a host of whimsical creatures, fulfilling Lisa's wish that the journal have the feel of a "wild and foreign city."

Even those artists who found the color well outside their usual palette got into the swim of things. Soon they were floating through the aqua sky and swimming in the aqua sea.

SAILING BOATS AND SHIPS

bout; 4, Chesapeake Bay bugeye; 5, sloop
1, bark; 12, hermaphrodite brig; 13, barken

DREAM
D
DESTINY
DISCOVER

MMMM
NNNNI
NOSS

Aqua

A seaside afternoon,
a pretty party dress,
butterfly wings.
Celestial visions.
Aqua inspires images
of flight and fancy.

carries me
away. Floating
is as close
as I will
come to
flying,
body

45c AUSTRALIA

es y Dorniro Ga

dreamy

eathing's

nd the

Forget-me-not

Aqua Exotica was created when my first book, Forest Floor, ended up missing in action. I called Lynne and offered to do a new book. It looked like Forest Floor was gone. We decided to go forward with a second journal, and because Aqua would be a few weeks behind in the rotation, the colorists were asked to give it the "priority green light" until it caught up. I was very sad about the loss of Forest Floor, so I decided to completely switch gears. Forest Floor had been rich, elegant and earthy. I needed a color that represented the other extreme. I needed the feeling of lightness and space—the sky, filled with aqua.

Forest Floor was fairly large, and my Aqua journal would be smaller for two reasons:
—A smaller book tends to move through the artists' hands at a faster pace.
—I wanted the book to feel, well, sassy.

I went for a kitschy, wacky approach. I created the name Aqua Exotica with the idea that readers would feel as though they had entered a wild and foreign city, a bit like the bar scene in the first *Star Wars* movie. As for the cover, I popped on a sequin for that funky, trashy look, and added a red rose for contrast against the beautiful color. I had to mix up my own paint recipe to get the perfect shade of aqua. The black burlap paper created a nice textural contrast. I created an inside pocket and asked the colorists to make and insert their own passport before entering. Aqua Exotica ended up being the eccentric, wild and impulsive cousin of Forest Floor. Within a matter of weeks, Forest Floor re-surfaced, and we all breathed a sigh of relief. I had a party.

This project came at a very good time. My studio was in boxes due to the move to a bigger space, and suddenly I was given the incentive I needed to open the boxes and organize quickly. Of course, it was a pleasure and an honor to be included in such an amazing group of artists, so the motivation and excitement was high.

I happen to be an art supply-junkie, so after closing my rubber stamp/art supply store, I was up to my teeth in samples of this and that, anxious to crack everything open and get going. The *True Colors* project gave me the perfect opportunity to play with all of it. This situation provided me with the approach that re-emerged throughout the project: I would see the next book and a concept and design would pop into my head. Sometimes just knowing which book was on the way would start the wheels turning.

***

I loved opening every new box and taking time to pore over each journal with awe. My family started to recognize the works of various artists as the project progressed. I can remember keeping each book in a very special place, safe from curious hands, dog teeth and an accidental spill. Each book took on the significance of the Holy Grail and was treated as such. If there had been a house fire, those books would have been within easy reach as we flew out the door! Occasionally, I would meet a friend for coffee and bring the current book. As I pulled out the piece, a crowd would gather and gasp, asking a million questions. People from every walk of life were drawn in by the beauty and diversity of each book. This was a delightful reminder that we were involved in something truly magical and extraordinary!

***

As I would sit down to work on a journal, the supplies and materials that called to me would often alter, poke, prod or completely change the original concept. There were several times when I would get up hours later to see a piece of work that had absolutely nothing to do with the original concept. This was very exciting and liberating. I could now trust myself to simply create, and turn off the critic and self-editor. There were only a couple of times when the work of the originating artist or previous colorists influenced my final piece. I might look at a new book and think, "This is looking very, very sweet. Let's stir the pot a little and toss in something risky and a little weird." I would take the chance and go for it.

I felt a rare pang of self-doubt only on a page or two, when my finished product was extremely simple graphically. I would wonder if I should continue layering and adding so that the page looked more "worked." Well, hours later, after re-working that piece to within an inch of its life, I would invariably toss it and re-create the original, loving it all the more for its straight-forward approach.

—Lisa Hoffman

Aqua

Aqua Exotica ... such serendipity! What a fun and unexpected treat to add to our project. This charmer is a cool size, and its name alone implies play. I eventually decided on a seaside theme with vintage postcard imagery that just begged to be 3-D. I popped out the gang in beach attire with pieces of foam core—love those striped suits! The babe languishing on the sand needed a sun hat, so I grabbed a scrap of paper on my drafting table. It just happened to be text about types of ships, so of course it instantly became her tricorn chapeau.

—Judi Riesch

TYPES OF SAILING BOATS AND SHIPS
; 3, knockabout; 4, Chesapeake Bay bugeye; 5, sloop; 6, ya
10, brig; 11, bark; 12, hermaphrodite brig; 13, barkentine.

by the beau-ti-ful sea

292.

j. riesch 5/2002

Artist: Marylinn Kelly

Advance word about Aqua had me thinking about the 1950s, an era of turquoise convertibles and boomerang-shaped coffee tables. When the book arrived, however, my thoughts moved in another direction. There were so many interpretations of aqua, beginning with the cover. For several years, I have taken an "Aqua" aerobics class from April through October; I spend hours a week immersed in water. Since the first session, the feeling of freedom that weightlessness brings has affected me deeply. Add to that some butterfly postage stamps left by my father, and I had wings and weightlessness for my entry. The two spoke to me of hope, so the words on my pages refer to defying gravity, to float and soar, illustrated by winged creatures.

—Marylinn Kelly

By the time I received the Aqua journal, it was already bulging with contributions. I decided to make a quilted fabric spread that was an exercise in French knots. I did some free-motion machine embroidery that covered the background in a squiggly pattern, added a quote done in stem stitch and some appliqués, then covered the surface with French knots in different shades of aqua and a touch of red. I love the way the texture feels when you run your hand over it.

—Keely Barham

Artist: Keely Barham

AQUA carries me away. Floating is as close as I will come to flying, body suspended...

continued... toes up and almost weightless in the sheer turquoise of the swimming pool. If even for one moment I a separate from the Earth.

continued like a... from the fri... anything be impossible

pulled ca...

Artist: Marylinn Kelly

This journal was unlike any of the others. It was small and chunky and playful, almost like a teenage diary. It seemed to ask for whimsical ideas, and my biggest problem was sorting through the hundreds of possibilities. Finally, I decided it should be a celebration of girls. Charm bracelets, polka dots, beehive hairdos, 45 rpm records, taffeta skirts, and makeup. After taking Anne Bagby's class, I found a new appreciation for stencils and the use of positive/negative images. So one Xerox image of the "girl group" could literally be used two different ways, allowing polka dot stenciling to unite the two pages and add patterning. I enjoyed using a rubber stamp of a charm bracelet and creating a faux bracelet of metallic braid and trinkets.

By the time I got this journal, it had all kinds of insertions that extended out beyond the covers. I decided to continue the fun with an old 45 rpm record, painted in the appropriate color and stuffed into a jacket with tulle netting. Frou-frou, silly and feminine. After finishing these pages, I wanted to visit a vintage dime store, hang around the cosmetics counter, then go have four-for-a-quarter pictures taken in the booth, over by the popcorn machine.

—Lynne Perrella

I started with a watercolor wash of aqua paint. The robe is made from bright aqua and orange hand-marbled papers that unfold to reveal a blue moon made from polymer clay. It is encased inside a wire mesh house with doors that can open wide.

—Lisa Renner

Aqua

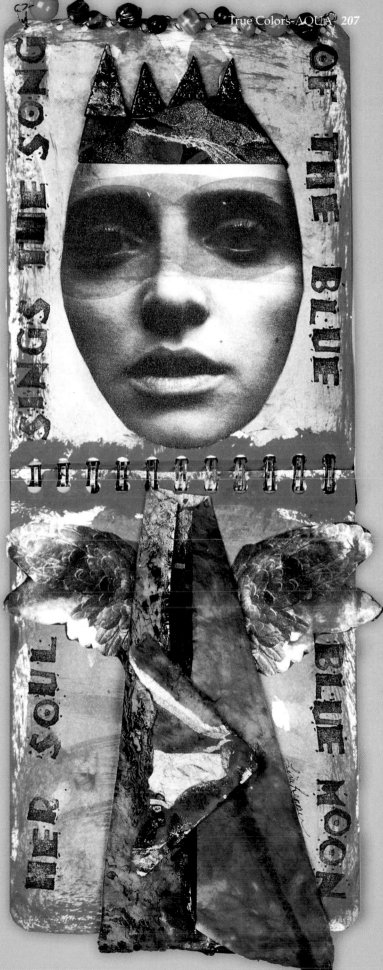

"soon she won't object to fingers that stray under her skirt hem and linger at her lightly knotted

This little journal seemed to have an erotic feeling—or maybe it was just me that day. I did these collages a few years ago, but they seemed to go with the quote I found for my entry. The background is wax resist under watercolor. I was not able to stick with one color—I had to add something for contrast.

—Teesha Moore

waistband; when
her eyes are dreamy
and her breathing's
harsh, send the
servants away."

—Mallyana Vatsyayana
(2nd century)

Aqua

When I got Lisa Hoffman's Aqua Exotica journal, I went into an art-making frenzy. I did eight or nine pages—but who's counting? I noticed there were lots of empty pages, and I thought that I was one of the last artists to work on the book, so I considered it my duty to fill it up.

When my neighbors moved, they asked me to throw out a lot of stuff for them. Because I have a hard time throwing away anything that might come in handy "someday," a decaying silk hanky, a perfect aqua color, became further art fodder in Aqua Exotica. It is now the stream from a smokestack on a postcard ocean liner. One person's trash is truly another person's treasure.

—Monica Riffe

and then she saw him

mary mary
quite contrary
how does your
garden
GROW?

Lisa Renner's journal combines the cool of blue with the warmth of ochre.

What is ochre? To Marylinn Kelly, ochre is an "artist's word." "Where does it ever appear," she wonders, "except in the context of art?" The artists defined ochre as a scrap of gold joss paper on an abstract collage, a background streaked with reddish-brown paint, a drawing of a golden girl. Blue could be, well, anything: A blue sky. A blueprint. A blue mood.

Lisa's love of texture can be seen—and felt—on her journal. Layers of gel medium, tissue paper, paint, and even a swatch of fabric made it onto her cover. Her tactile approach to her journal proved contagious.

The pages of this spiral-bound journal are stiff with layer upon layer of assorted mediums. Monica Riffe painted her background sky with a coat of blue acrylic thick enough for her to scratch out the words "blue and ochre." Karen Michel painted puffy clouds on a turquoise sky to frame a photograph she'd taken of the passing desert in Santa Fe, New Mexico.

Karen says it best: "This book evoked the earth and sky."

Blue & Ochre

Ochre houses and blue skies.
A golden portrait,
and a blue jeans sun.
A color combination
that mystifies and delights.

I can't say I have a favorite color—I love them all. I initially chose blue because it had not been selected by anyone in our group. Although I love blue, I normally don't work much with it in my art, so my other reason for choosing it was to have my journal reflect a color that is apart from my norm. I knew immediately that I wanted to combine blue with ochre and work with a slightly complementary color theme. Blue evokes a calmness, a serene passion in me. Ochre radiates warmth, and together they create a balanced contrast that flows.

***

I enjoy working with all kinds of interesting texture techniques. Texture stimulates both the visual and tactile senses. To enhance the cover of my journal, I used a gel medium and tissue paper to produce a thick, slightly rough surface. I had painted some fabric using blue and yellow, and I embedded a piece of it in the wet medium. When it dried, I layered acrylic paint in shades of ochre and burnt sienna all over the textured surface. The title for my journal, "Color My World," came to me instantly. First, it is the title to a song from the '70s that I still love by Chicago. (Does anyone else remember it being played at the school dance?) Second, it was the perfect invitation for each artist to make her personal mark on those pristine pages.

The face on the front is made of polymer clay using one of the many molds I have collected. (My most infamous face-molding experience occurred while I was in Paris on vacation. I had taken polymer clay with me to make molds of interesting faces. The hotel where we were staying had two beautiful chairs in the lobby. The arms of the chairs sported a stoic Grecian, brass face on each, which I noticed immediately when we were checking in. I went to my room and rolled several balls of clay, placed them in a cigar box, and proceeded down to the lobby. I took a seat in one of the chairs and waited. When the front desk staff wasn't looking, I quickly pressed each ball of clay on the brass face, then carefully removed them so my molds would be perfect. I came home with several molds for my friends. It was great.)

***

I was thrilled to be a part of this project and enamored with the idea of working with such talented women, who shared their art so freely. *True Colors* was set up for each of us to mail our journal to an artist, who then had two weeks to work on it before mailing it to the next person on the list. The cycle continued so that every two weeks we received another journal in which to leave our artistic mark. At first I was concerned that I wouldn't be able to keep up, but I soon realized that having that small window of time actually stimulated me and kept things lively and fresh.

The key to the success of such a massive endeavor is having unwavering organization from the outset—my thanks to Lynne for her incredible and diplomatic efforts. I felt that, as artists, we were considerate of each other, and if one of us came up against a time constraint when trying to meet deadlines, we found a way to work around her. It was a collaborative effort in every sense of the word, and I thank every one of these artists for their patience and generosity.

Because a theme such as color is broad and almost free of boundaries, it left plenty of room for artistic interpretation. Each color evoked diverse emotions, and as each journal arrived, it was met with a new challenge and a new approach, resulting in unique creative resolve. It was amazing.

—Lisa Renner

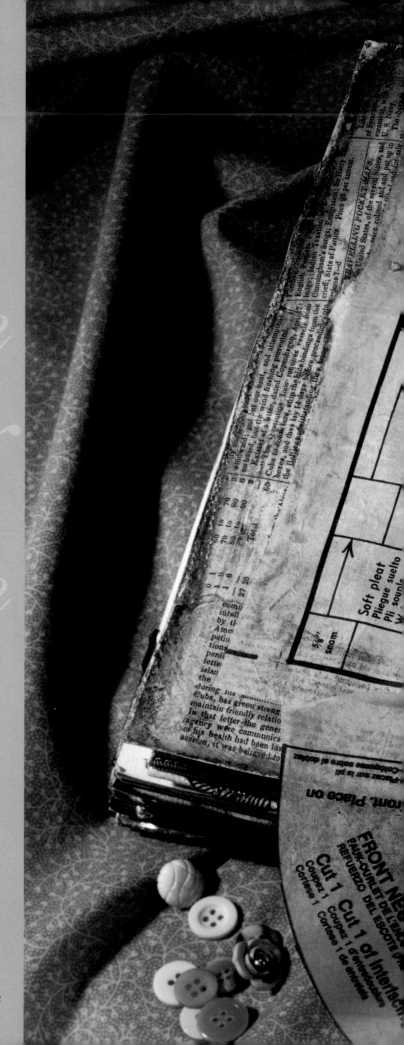

Blue

&

Ochre

Working in Lisa's journal was a real turning point for my artwork. It was my first experiment with melding my own drawings into my collages. It reminded me of how I used to create my collages when I first made them eight years ago. Starting with a dress pattern (my all-time favorite background), I drew in oil pastel on top, then glued buttons and various other collage papers. Probably not my best work ever, but I really felt like this piece marked a new beginning in the way that I want to work.
                                              —Claudine Hellmuth

Artist: Anne Bagby

Oh yes, the House of True Colors. Did I mention that the *Blue & Ochre* journal was one of my favorites? This color way had me a little perplexed until I looked down at a huge stack of blueprints, and the light popped on! Luckily, the man in my life is an architect, so I knew I had the concept nailed. The tricky part was that I didn't know the players very well because the project was still new. I had to think about the communications we had shared as a group, the work I had seen in the books thus far, and any scrap of information I had about each person. This was really going out on a limb: Each building part corresponded with a particular artist. We based the actual "House" on a turn-of-the-century home that Jim uses as his architectural studio. The rest of the layout included paint swatches and little images that fed into the story of the House of True Colors. I included an old skeleton key with the phrase "Here's Your Key," hoping that each artist would feel a connection to the house and each other.
—Lisa Hoffman

Blue & Ochre

Lisa's journal was the first I received as the project got under way. I remember how exciting it was to open the long-anticipated parcel. The large spiral-bound book, collaged with wonderful textured papers, set just the tone I expected from Lisa. It was difficult to decide how to approach this first entry. The color issue was not daunting for me, because I was comfortable using the more subtle shades of ochre and a deep turquoise blue. I finally chose to use a very simple but unusual cabinet card of six women, bust views, with the same sash over their shoulder. I layered paints and pieces of a Mexican newspaper on my pages, then created a positive/negative design, repeating and reversing the images in a series of squares. Over-painting and stamping added some depth to these two-dimensional pages.
—Judi Riesch

The colors for this page suited me, and the patterns and image went down without any problem. It was liberating to use both pages and work in a large format. I began with the form of Daisy Buchanan, but decided she was too dark for Daisy. Still, it was a cautionary tale: All that glitters is not gold.
—Anne Bagby

Artist: Lisa Hoffman

Artist: Judi Riesch

THERE'S A LADY WHO'S SURE

ALL THAT GLITTERS IS GOLD

AND SHE'S BUYING A

STAIRWAY TO HEAVEN

WHEN SHE GETS THERE SHE KNOWS

IF THE STORES ARE ALL CLOSED

WITH A WORD SHE CAN GET

WHAT SHE CAME FOR

AND SHE'S BUYING A

STAIRWAY TO HEAVEN

I loved seeing Lisa's journal with her handsome cover of textured color. I adore ochre, but blue presented a challenge to my comfort palette. I had an English postage stamp of an angel in royal blue robes with a golden halo that I wanted to incorporate. While searching for a piece of music to inspire me, I came upon "Stairway to Heaven" by Led Zeppelin, which prompted my journal entry. I built a shrine with a pull-down staircase, using the lyrics to the song on the risers leading up to the angel stamp. Then I had fun creating mock classified ads of stairways for sale, playing off the line "she's buying a stairway to heaven." A mini-CD recording accompanies the journal. As it turned out, I didn't even use ochre but chose metallic gold in place of it.

—Michelle Ward

Artist: Marylinn Kelly

Ochre is, to me, such an artist's word. Where does it ever appear, except in the context of art? The word had me thinking about images of or from other art sources. The figure I used is from a calendar of traditional illustrations and featured my interpretation of the colors. I then added tinted tags with objects I hoped would be examples of the Rumi quote, "Each thing in the Universe is a vessel full to the brim with wisdom and beauty." Some lithographed tin bug pins, a piece of shrink art and millinery supplies are glued over a background created by painting, dripping, sponging, rubbing, and spattering.
—*Marylinn Kelly*

Blue & Ochre

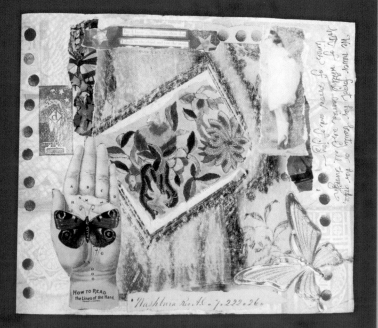

Artist: Nina Bagley

Here I used a butterfly theme that sent me spinning yet another magical story of a gypsy girl who "smelled of honey and the sea." For two or three years I had been saving a magnificent antique square of intricately embroidered silk cloth, taken from a Chinese sash for a robe, and decided that Lisa's journal would be just the canvas for the fabric's focal point. I had also saved an image from a magazine of a young girl holding a frame— a girl wearing a lovely golden sequined dress. She's what I imagined a queenly gypsy girl would have for her special court. Out came the golden butterflies, along with another story of unforgettable visits to a village by a magical young gypsy girl who was courted by butterflies.
—*Nina Bagley*

I was inspired by this color scheme. Anything with yellow (especially golden yellow) truly gets me going. I just played on the pages, treating Lisa's journal as if it were my own. The only thing it needed in my eyes was the finishing touch of journal writing.
—*Teesha Moore*

Artist: Lynne Perrella

I could understand Lisa's love affair with this combination of colors, and I was tempted to try a page of abstract applied color without any specific central visual element or text. As I layered the colors, however, and added wisps of tissue paper and handmade Oriental papers, I realized how much the design looked like a dreamlike sky. I decided to include gift-wrap images of star charts and astrological signs, and I soon realized that the composition was beginning to suggest a stage set or a backdrop for a drama. Judi had given me some printed tissue paper of

Raphael paintings, so the noblemen and princes were collaged into place. All they seemed to need were the two rival queens. I liked finding the little pieces of paper lace to "dress" the minimally clad ladies, and enjoyed the way the final pages seemed to announce an opera or Shakespearean tragedy. The strength of the pages seemed to rely on the densely painted and layered backdrop, with the graphic and poster-like images of the queens. Let the play begin!

—Lynne Perrella

Artist: Teesha Moore

I never realized how often blue and ochre show up together in the world, until I focused on the duo as I looked for inspiration to begin work on Lisa Renner's book.

The houses on my pages are from a pop-up card depicting Monet's home. Lynne Perrella sent the card to me years ago. For the back pocket in this book, I also made a house-shaped tag. I included a page from my ABC of Color book, with a description of complementary colors. At the time, I was experimenting with scratching through a layer of acrylic paint, down to a layer that was sealed by gel medium. So I spelled out "blue and ochre" in this way on my pages.

Working in tandem on Lisa Renner's Blue & Ochre book, Lisa Hoffman and I made some dangly beaded elements for its cover. We also replaced the original wire binding with copper wire. To us, it looked like it wanted a little more embellishment, and a new funky binding wire to complement the rich textural surface Lisa Renner had created. After her book was returned to her, Lisa wrote that she approved of what we had done. I'm glad, because it was rather bold of us!

—Monica Riffe

COLORS
General
Lesson
Lesson
Lesson
Lesson 5 Complementary colors
Lesson 6 Complementary tones
blue and ochre

SIMPLE...

K·MICHEL

Blue & Ochre

This book evoked the earth and sky. I used to live in New Mexico, and this color combination immediately reminded me of the desert landscape. I fished out a photo I took while in Santa Fe, along with some imagery one would expect to find in a traveler's journal. A very simple word came to mind while working in Lisa's journal: "Roam."

—*Karen Michel*

Lisa Renner's journal contains my favorite entry from the entire project. I absolutely loved Michelle Ward's "Stairway to Heaven" pages. They just took my breath away. For my entry, I had some blue and yellow sun theme fabric in my stash that I pulled out to use for my background. I had a face under glass that I had already beaded with blue seed beads, so I thought it was perfect to use as a doll's head. I made the doll and accent pieces with leftover denim from a jeans jacket. I frayed some of the exposed edges on the denim for a rustic look.

—Keely Barham

A love of vintage photographs, letters and other old things inspired Judi Riesch to choose sepia for her color. Her choice of journal also reflects her love of the past; it's an antique leather book that she altered and filled with watercolor paper. On the cover, Judi added tiny glass vials containing bits of paper or paint in her color scheme that look like the ingredients to a secret, long-lost potion. The result: A journal that resembles a rescued artifact, one filled with ancient charms, wit and wisdom.

In keeping with the theme, the artists embellished their entries with photographs of ancestors, aged paper, lace, buttons, and other sepia-colored ephemera. Yet the way they assembled their images gave these vintage finds a contemporary twist. Consider Lisa Renner's edgy pages, with their wire-wrapped metal and unlikely combination of elements. Add a domino to a page with a picture of a winged medieval beauty? Only an artist would think to do it, and it works.

Linn Jacobs liked the Sepia journal because of its "layers and layers of stuff to touch, all inviting me to think about other times and places." Indeed, this journal effectively blends remnants of the past with modern artistic sensibilities.

Sepia

Old photographs.
Coffee-stained paper.
The crushed walnut juice of a
calligrapher's ink. Sepia.
Even the word is lovely…

For my journal, I chose sepia—soft browns, oatmeal, buff, ecru, walnut, chestnut, the color of vintage photographs, the warm brown tones of the earth. This quote from *The Spring of Joy* (1917) by Mary Webb says it all: "Of all colors Brown is the most satisfying. It is the deep fertile tint of the Earth itself." I suppose these hues were my comfort zone, so there was no question about my choice of journal color. For as long as I can remember, collecting old photos, albums, documents, letters, and many other kinds of ephemera has constantly fueled my creativity, and their colors became my palette.

***

Several years ago, I purchased a small group of books that had their pages removed to sell the engravings. With covers and spines intact, they were just too lovely to cut apart. One of these volumes, a lovely, age-worn leather book, was the perfect choice for my journal—so warm and inviting. I removed the spine and purchased my favorite paper to work on—140-pound Hot Press watercolor paper. I am not a bookbinder, so I enlisted the help of a good friend to coptic-bind the book.

I wanted the cover art to be simple so it would not take away from the beauty of the leather. I decided to layer on another cover, one of an old cabinet card photo album with its brass clasps still attached. A daguerreotype case holds tiny glass vials lined up like soldiers, each one containing a snippet of paper or a bit of paint in my color range. I loved the texture of the corks and the small number labels that implied such an amazing range of possibilities within the choice of sepia! A piece of a tintype as well as an old metal indexing tab are the only other additions to the front of the journal. The inside covers of the journal have a fabulous marbled end paper with the original owner's bookplate label still attached. Using photos and Polaroid image transfers, handmade papers and pieces of leather spines, I tried to set the tone for this Sepia journal before it began its journey.

***

When I agreed to join Lynne Perrella's color journal project, I was a bit nervous. I was accustomed to collaborating with other artists, but never on this scale—15 artists! Not only would I be creating in all of their journals, but in living color. For me, this would be a major challenge because I work primarily in warm earth tones. In addition, I was not a regular keeper of art journals. I occasionally dabble in creating pages in a "sometimes" journal, and this project became a terrific creative outlet for me—a place to try new techniques, papers and colors and to add new depth to ideas. I saw it as an opportunity to learn from other artists in this unfamiliar territory of color.

Each book's arrival was truly an event. Occasionally I would tear open the box before the postman drove away, but more often than not I would wait until later, using the unveiling as a treat or incentive to stay on task during the day. With coffee or wine in hand, I would savor each and every detail of the journals. I loved how they gradually began looking so full—they spilled out of all sides with ribbons, fibers, charms, beads—even mini CDs ala Michelle. The overflow was just a preview of the incredible details within.

Sometimes I knew exactly what the approach would be for my entry, but other times I would agonize for days hoping the universe would provide the inspiration I needed. What I call the gathering process has always been integral to my work. Usually I would collect things—photos, papers or objects—and eventually they would find their way into my art. For the *True Colors* project, however, I thought about the journals on each shopping trip or outing; I was always looking for just the right ribbon for the Violet & Yellow journal or a paper destined for the Red journal. I also found myself buying a myriad of paint colors, something I had never done before. As the time neared for the journals to be sent home, my excitement grew. The other artists were receiving their journals and posting e-mails to our group, and at that time I found a great little poem that seemed to suit the moment. I shared it in an e-mail:

"Sweet is the hour that brings us home,
Where all will spring to meet us;
Where hands are striving, as we come,
To be the first to greet us."
—Eliza Cook, 1848

When Sepia finally completed its journey home I was incredibly touched and overcome by the generous work of this wonderful group of artists. Each and every page, each and every woman, a gift.

—Judi Riesch

I didn't have a clear path in mind when I started painting watercolor on the background for the Sepia journal pages. On one side, I started doodling leaves and branches, which eventually became a sepia tree. I then added the fabric butterfly lady, which I hand-quilted with a tiny running stitch. I framed the fabric piece with a darker brown watercolor fabric, then glued the finished quilt onto one of the pages.

—Keely Barham

Artist: Judi Riesch

Working in sepia was a fun change from all the other bright colors. If anyone can do sepia, it's Judi. She knows how to work those browns and not end up with a muddy mess! For this journal, I was playing with cardboard stencils from the hardware store. I used the number 8 and added a little paint to distress it. I collaged it on top of a collage of a woman that I had already created, then scanned and glued it into Judi's book. I gave the entire page a wash of light ochre to blend it together.

—Claudine Hellmuth

Artist: Claudine Hellmuth

Artist: Lisa Hoffm

The first book that I received in this project was Sepia. Its arrival was the perfect initiation into the world of True Colors and the next year of my life! The quality of work was astounding, and the bar was high. I actually started with the concept of using a knife. The layout was to include the phrase "Art at the Cutting Edge." As I held the book, I felt that the tone of the work should be less "cheeky" and more elegant. The knife was given to me by a friend and had a touch of wonderful paint-work done in an Oriental style. Playing with that theme, I let the work evolve into a mini-story about the journey of a family from the mainland to their home in the New World. The image of a smiling mother and son was transferred onto an old linen towel. Their expressions are filled with joy and hope, so I included a map that showed a section of California that has a large Asian population. This was to be their destination. The shell and rose imagery conveys happiness and adventure. As I finished these pages, I realized that the original knife held little significance, except to lend an interesting visual element to the layout.

—Lisa Hoffman

I had a few doubts about working in this book. It has a subdued palette that I don't usually choose of my own free will. I liked what I did, though—my pages remind me of a scrapbook a young girl might keep who has gone off to the Windy City—Chicago. There are photos with friends, a little journaling and some lovely lyrics she might have heard somewhere. I also combined ornate little metal findings with rough cloth on these pages, another pleasing juxtaposition.

—Sarah Fishburn

Artist: Sarah Fishburn

Receiving Judi's journal was very intimidating, with its gorgeous cover and assemblage of sepia elements, because Judi is the Master of Sepia. My soundtrack began with a few classic tunes: "Easter Parade," "Mr. Sandman," "Dream a Little Dream," and one contemporary song that I know Judi loves, "I Hope You Dance." For one journal page, I scanned my own wedding photos and turned them into sepia to match my grandparents' photo. On this page, I inserted a written message about following an English tradition, told to us by my mother-in-law, of leaving your bouquet on the grave of a loved one. The day after my wedding, we visited my grandmother at the cemetery and left her my flowers in remembrance. Another journal page began as a tribute to fancy Easter bonnets and New York's Fifth Avenue. I selected sepia cabinet card copies of women in wide-brimmed hats, and I found a postcard of a young cameraman to complete the lyric, "the photographers will snap us." Mounted next to him is a four-leafed clover with additional song lines ("I'll be all in clover"). As an extension of this page, I created a mini-book as a milliner's swatch record, with a haberdashery appointment card, to dangle from the journal.

—Michelle Ward

Sepia

HARLEQUIN AND COLUMBINE AND PIERROT,
MIMED THEIR WAY INTO THESE HEARTS
BECAUSE THEY BROUGHT WITH THEM CENTURIES
OF NOSTALGIA, TRAGICOMIC EMOTIONS,
HIDDEN TERRORS, AND YEARNINGS.

COLUMBINE, WILD AND TRUE AND BEAUTIFUL BEAST. . . CREATED TO STIR UP GREAT
DISASTER, TO LURE, SEDUCE AND POISON. WEEKIND

Artist: Anne Bagby

Artist: Marylinn Kelly

Judi sent photos of her book-within-a-book so I could get a sense of Sepia. I had already been picturing old photos and seeing some of the other pages strengthened that feeling. But what else? I took my cue from the photo I selected, a studio portrait of a no-nonsense faux ancestor, her bonnet tightly tied, her cloak firmly fastened. From that image came "Button up your overcoat," along with vintage buttons and lace, over a painted background that I stamped with hand-carved stamps. It was the sort of advice our grandparents were always giving us, and it left me feeling connected to generations of solid women I never knew.

—Marylinn Kelly

I liked Judi's choice of colors, and I suspected it was a good choice for a group effort. Using neutrals meant that the colors would not clash. Because Judi uses these colors all the time, her presence seemed to resonate throughout this book. Columbine was a continuation of my interest in the Commedia del arte. The woman I drew didn't look wild, but she looked liberated and strong. I would love to see this book as a finished product—I just saw it at the beginning and even then it was spectacular.

—*Anne Bagby*

I had so much fun with this journal. I shopped for an antique photo that spoke to me and added some bits from an antique car parts box I found while cleaning out my old studio. The shorter inner pages provided me with a different format to play with, which gave me another perspective to add to my page spread.

—*Karen Michel*

Layer by incredible layer, Judi Reisch's Sepia journal, wrapped like a present in tea-stained cloth and tied with a bow, was such a visual gift. Hers was the first journal I had to work in, and the quality of this book set the stage for excellence. What a dramatic beginning to the True Colors project!

—*Monica Riffe*

Artist: Karen Michel

Artist: Monica Riffe

WOMAN'S

a

I started working on the Sepia journal by coffee-staining my pages. The inspiration for the use of copper mesh came from a class I took from the lovely Nina Bagley. I used it to make pockets attached with eyelets. I inserted copper to show behind the mesh. A fold-out page, made from watercolor paper, was also attached with eyelets and rubber-stamped with various block designs (Post Modern, Stampers Anonymous, Judi-Kins). On the last page, I color-copied the female image onto acetate and backed it with a section of copper. Copper tape that I antiqued with liver of sulphur surrounds the edge of the acetate. I wrote the poem in honor of this entire group of women, who have poured their creative hearts into this project.

—Lisa Renner

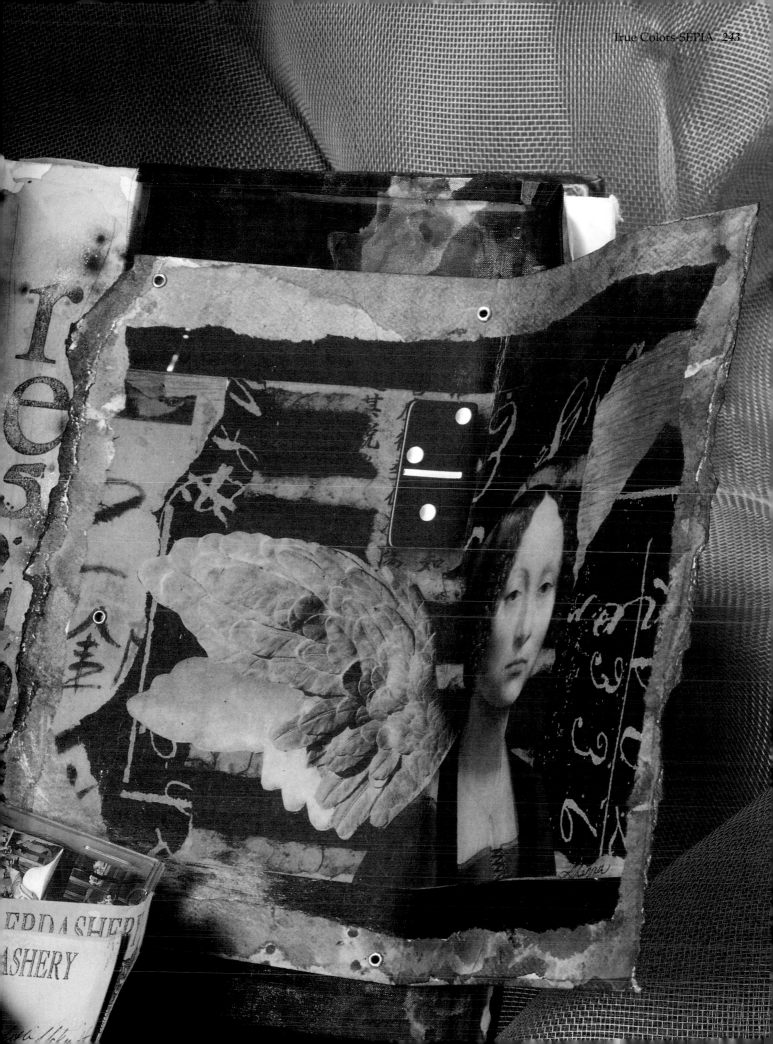

Sepia & The Telling Detail

When I hear the word "sepia", there is one image that inevitably comes to mind: the old well-loved group photo taken of my longago family at a family reunion. There they stand, amongst the tall weeds and tangled shrub of someone's backyard. Over their shoulders, a sturdy clapboard house with a shallow porch can be seen. But....for me.....the lure of the photo is in the faces. Everyone of these dear souls are departed now. The very last one to die, Lee Young, passed away just a couple of years ago. Goodness, he must have been a very old man. The familiar family nicknames trip through my mind as I skim the faces -- Buss, Ode, Ran, Mammy, Mayme, Fad. No wonder I have longed for a nickname all my life......But the only one that ever "stuck" was Dollbaby, and only Dad called me that. There is Dad, that little angelic-looking boy in the front row; proving how deceptive a photo can be. Dad never wasted a moment of his long life being angelic -- and in fact was one of the most uproarious Kendall boys ever. No wonder there is that worried look on his mother's face, there in the back row. She stands shoulder-to-shoulder with her also-worrisome husband, Randolph. Tell me something about him, I would always plead to my father. "Well, all I remember is......(big dramatic pause) he'd beat the hell out of me." That's all he'd say about his own tall, rangy, raw-boned father. Randolph Kendall came north from Virginia, with his younger brother, Oscar, and they both took jobs on the King Farm, in Unity. They say that Ran took one

Sepia

Sewing and fabric are not my thing, and yet I adore the look of quilts and respect the tradition of quilt-making. From a graphic design point of view, I have always loved the challenge of setting up a grid and filling in the spaces, finding the right balance of light and dark. It was with the love of quilts and grids and family lore that I began these pages in Judi's journal. I had a warm kindred response to the cover of her book and her introductory pages. They were done with such skill and love of antiquity that I wanted to continue the feeling, but in my own way. I wanted my pages to have the traditional look of a quilt, but the modern appreciation for design and balance, and I wanted to add a story about my family. Using a vintage family reunion photo, I decided to sprinkle the various wonderful faces throughout the "quilt" then (in a sense) unite them all together in the story. I raided my paper drawers for sepia bits and pieces, and was surprised at how few turned up. In the end, the very last blocks of the grid were filled in with not-quite-sepia papers that had to be tea-stained, and I came away, yet again, fully appreciative of Judi's mastery of that wonderful regal realm, sepia.

—Lynne Perrella

Keely Barham chose black because, well, no one else did. And a project called *True Colors* would be remiss without black.

She calculated, correctly, that black would get the artists asking the deeper questions, probing the darker side of life—and mortality. A talented fabric artist, Keely created a funereal cover made of black velvet embroidered with a cross, and sent the pillow-soft book on its way. Black prompted the artists to create somber images of women in mourning, dark skies and foreboding crows. Still, not everyone thought of cemeteries and scary things.

"What black suggested to me was not mourning or Halloween, though they crossed my mind, but the blacktop of the highway," writes Marylinn Kelly, whose entry recalls her childhood road trips. The artists also found beauty in black. Judi Riesch's cemetery scene is hauntingly lovely, while Anne Bagby's portrait of an African-American woman, with its subtle dark hues, is understated elegance.

Lest anyone still think black is boring, consider the intriguing entry by Lisa Renner. Lisa uses black acrylic paint, eyelets, torn window screen, feathers and even chicken wire to create an homage to Paul McCartney's song, "Blackbird." Paint it black, indeed.

The culture of th
the lure of the h
Blacktop and a wh
Roadside attracti
open country, sma
Drive all night.
to coast.
unnels,

Black

Black lace and bra straps.
A funeral veil and film noir.
Come on over to the dark side,
and see how colorful
black can be …

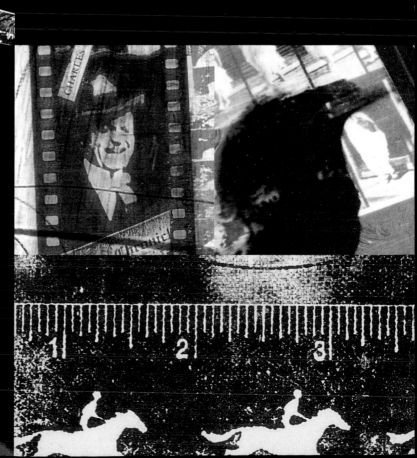

I chose black for my journal because I thought none of the other artists would choose it, and I felt that we really needed to have black in the mix. I also felt everyone would have fun creating in black and exploring some darker issues. I envisioned lots of gothic-inspired artwork. I seem to have an affinity with the color black. I am drawn to it when I am shopping for clothes, and I must have about 25 different pairs of black shoes.

***

For the journal cover, I knew I wanted to make something in fabric, and I wanted to convey to the group that gothic feeling. I gathered all of the black fabric and trims from my fabric stash that I could find and decided to make a kind of crazy quilt for the back cover. For the front, I had recently drawn a gothic-looking cross with intertwining vines for a graphics project and thought it would be a good focal point. I machine-embroidered the outline of the cross with black thread on black velvet. When I had the journal put together, I drew the word "black" in a calligraphic style on cardstock and glued it under a large squashed marble. I used black seed beads and peyote-stitched around the glass. When finished, I glued it over the cross.

***

I was thrilled to be asked to participate in this collaboration. I love working this way—sharing with other artists and seeing the different ways each one of us creates. I was a little nervous about the actual journaling because I do not keep journals regularly (I'm embarrassed to admit) and working in paper arts is not my strongest area. I tried to stick to paper collage for the first few journals I worked on, but by the fourth or fifth journal I switched over to my comfort zone—fabric—and started making art quilts for each of my journal entries. I felt much freer working this way and thought that I was able to give the other artists my best work.

—Keely Barham

This Journal belongs to: Keely Barham

66

"THERE CAN BE NO TRANSFORMING OF DARKNESS INTO LIGHT AND OF APATHY INTO MOVEMENT WITHOUT EMOTION"

Artist: Keely Barham

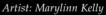

The Black journal reminds me how tactile all of the books were, how every cover and every page invited touching. Keely's sewn, fringed cover is an example. What black suggested to me was not mourning or Halloween, though they crossed my mind, but the blacktop of the highway. A piece of fine-grained black sandpaper is the backdrop for a miniature postcard album, photos and writings about the road. My influence was a combination of Jack Kerouac's On the Road and the years of car trips from my childhood. Oh, and all the hours spent at the drive-in.

—Marylinn Kelly

Artist: Marylinn Kelly

The culture of the road,
the lure of the highway.
Blacktop and a white line.
Roadside attractions,
open country, small towns.
Drive all night.
coast to coast.
tunnels, on we roll.
eyes open.

We all jumped to the music and agreed. The purity of the road. The white line in the middle of the highway unrolled and hugged our left front tire as if glued to our groove.

When this book came to me, I thought a lot about Keely's love of fabric and texture. I have not worked with quilting and have had little sewing experience, so I decided to focus on texture. I happened to pick up these bra extenders simply because I was stunned such a thing existed. The extenders became the grounding element for the layout. Going with the texture theme, I used a paint that had been roughened by using an acrylic additive. The fabric transfer photo lent itself to the romantic suggestion of black lingerie. I used a brightly colored, gypsy-beaded trim to frame out the bottom of the image. The glitter was very big and chunky—more texture that gave the piece a night-sky feeling. The roughly torn painted paper held a quote and was adhered with electrical tape. I hoped that Keely would see the kind of page that evoked the long and lazy strains of a solo saxophone, drifting over the hot and humid air of summer.

—Lisa Hoffman

Artist: Lisa Hoffman

Citizen Kane grabbed me the first time I saw it as a teenager, and I never tire of its angles, twists and turns. A masterpiece of odd perspectives and sharp contrasts in black and white, it includes strange portraits of people and animals, mixing the real and the surreal in each frame. I collaged elements together that hinted at the strangeness of the film, put them into a vertical filmstrip format, and made transparencies, which I glued to the page. The best part was replaying my favorite scenes from the movie as I worked. That is the real joy of journaling: To have those private moments of indulging our favorite images, while we spend time with ourselves.

—Lynne Perrella

Artist: Lynne Perrella

Artist: *Karen Michel*

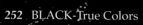

SHAPESHIFTER

CROW GIRL WATCHES CROW

Black

*K*eely's journal was the first one that I worked in. When I got her journal, it was so soft and fluffy. It felt like a pillow! My cat loved this journal. I constantly had to monitor her because she wanted to sit on top of it. Because of the beautiful velvet cover, I was scared to use any paint or glue in the actual book, so instead I decided to do a Gocco print (small screen printing machine) of a design I made on the computer. I secured the print to the page using eyelets.

—Claudine Hellmuth

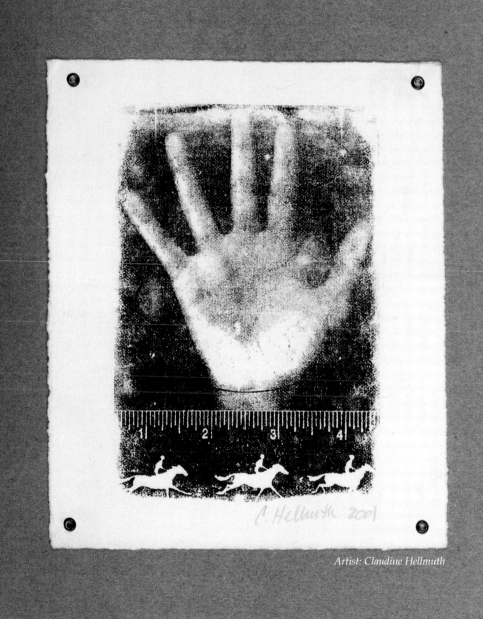

Artist: Claudine Hellmuth

*T*his book was beautifully mysterious, evoking secrets and dreams. I worked with Xeroxes and black and white inkjet print-outs to create images of crows.

—Karen Michel

The Black journal was one of my favorite books to play in!
Keely did an amazing job sewing her cover, and the black pages
were wonderful to work on. I received this journal in October
and had just finished reading Falling Angels by Tracy
Chevalier. This intriguing novel takes place in early 20th
century London, and much of the story involves a London
cemetery. I have always been drawn to cemetery statuary, so I
decided to do a spread with a Requiem theme. I became
fascinated with the details in the novel relating to funeral
customs of the time, and the large role that proper mourning
played in society. Everything from clothing for men, women
and children to jewelry and even stationery was very
specifically dictated by rules of etiquette. So with Andrew
Lloyd Weber's "Requiem" playing in my studio, I began. The
background of this entry is painted and collaged with pieces of
my Polaroid transfers from slides I have taken in various
cemeteries. I wanted to create an illusive atmosphere—soft and
moody. Using a full-length copy of a Victorian woman, I
sketched and colored over her clothing to give it a mourning
look. Various black feathers and vintage ribbon became a hat
and neckpiece on the portrait. After reading about the custom
of wearing pins with photos or hair of the dead loved one, I
fashioned a neckpiece with jewelry findings and a tintype. As a
last-minute addition, I laid a piece of black hat netting across
the entire spread.

—Judi Riesch

Black

As with all of my pages in the journals, nothing was ever calculated. I just sat down at my desk and started right in. Such was the case for Keely's journal. This figure just happened and the words for her popped into my head. Normally I would fill the pages with more stuff, but this seemed to be best left as it was. Sometimes I felt guilty about not spending as much time on one person's journal as I did another, but I just always followed the muse. This was one of my favorite pages.

—Teesha Moore

Black

Ah ... the power of black. The Black journal was fun in a dark, gothic way. McCartney's "Blackbird" came to mind and stuck as my theme. To begin, I used a brayer to apply black acrylic to the pages. I rubbed chalk in browns, yellows and purple over the dry paint. I like tactile art, so I made a booklet to be sewn in the middle of my page. I painted watercolor paper with black acrylics and tore around the edges to expose the white edge for effect. I then glued brown mulberry paper to the outside surface. A portion of McCartney's song lyrics was stamped inside. Pieces of window screen were sprayed black, then tacked to the front and back of the booklet with eyelets. For the facing page, I wanted the feather to appear as if it were floating, while the other collage elements appeared to be tied down. Chicken wire was sprayed black and layered with other paper elements for the dimensional effect.

—Lisa Renner

Because the color black is a strong, symbolic representation of identity for many Americans, I felt I could explore this idea by including a drawing of a person of color in the book—so I started with a drawing of an African-American woman. Instead of straight black, I used dark, nearly black blues.

—Anne Bagby

Coloring Outside the Lines
Artists' Tips and Techniques

by Linda Blinn

"The journals are exuberant and so full of stuff, I'm inspired to find a big old book and fill it up with everything I love."

We heard variations on this comment over and over while *True Colors* was in production here at Stampington & Company®. The journals delighted newspaper reporters, artists, photographers and our staff. Everyone who saw them just wanted to stay and play in the pages.

Many of the techniques in *True Colors* were a spontaneous combustion of expertise, inspiration and opportunity. An instructional "how-to" would diminish the purpose of this collaboration, which seeks to break rules rather than make them. Instead, we offer an overview of materials and techniques for your personal journey, so that you might discover your own true colors.

All That Glitters

The flash of a rhinestone, the glitter of sequins. Gold lamé and silver silk. Contrast counts, and so do details, no matter what the art form. Against a matte background, a mere hint of shimmer enlivens the entire page. For *True Colors*, glitz makes an appearance in the form of paper wings, moons, hearts, and butterflies, while ordinary metallic stars rise to the level of halos and, yes, even pasties. Diamonds may be a girl's best friend, but pearls and vintage jewelry can also win hearts as part of a collage composition.

TIPS

- Add pizzazz to pages with glitter.
- Anything metal brings contrast—even a brass door knocker.
- Religious metals and milagros are unexpected embellishments.
- Include small mirrors in different shapes.
- Use multiples or groups of shiny items.
- Add texture with foil, sequins, glass, and metallic threads.
- Tiny rhinestones can be used as eyes, buttons or halos.

as a child.

Pretty as
a Picture

SAILING BOATS AND SHIPS
about: 4, Chesapeake Bay bugeye; 5, sloop; 6,
11, bark; 12, hermaphrodite brig; 13, barkentin

It could be your grandmother in her wedding dress or a studio shot of a young immigrant, a risqué dancer or a grim matron. Whether they are images of relatives or absolute strangers, the milestones old pictures and photographs chronicle bring whimsy and nostalgia to the page. They often lead to recollections of lyrics to old songs and long-forgotten poems. A vintage photograph copied onto a transparency and placed over a background may become ethereal, poignant or even downright funny. By making small slits in the photograph you can have your subject may wave banners, clutch flowers or hold fast to a red balloon. Adding golden wings or a crown elevates mere mortals to angels and kings.

TIPS

- Combine vintage photos with contemporary ones sharing a similar pose or theme.
- Marilynn Kelly added old buttons and lace to her portrait of a woman with a firmly fastened coat and named her page "Button Up Your Overcoat."
- Cut out the person and place on foam core for a three-dimensional, paper doll effect. Judi Riesch's girls don colorful stockings and attend a party; others become bathing beauties in striped attire.
- Combine vintage school photographs with report cards, penmanship exercises and library cards in a collage. Brush with white gesso to soften.
- Affix photo corners and eyelets to make a pocket out of an old photograph.
- Enlarge photographs or reduce in size; use multiple copies of the same images in different sizes.
- Stamp on images or make into faux postage.

Layer It On

Some of the *True Colors* pages have more layers than an archaeological dig. Multiple coats of texture and layers of color entice the eyes to linger on a page. Close inspection may reveal a part, but not all of what lies beneath. How do the artists *do* that? Experiments done with a balance of confidence and abandon yield stunning results.

When describing what she does, Marilynn Kelly uses words like slather, sponge, splatter, splash, and scrub. She captured the movement and energy of the movie *Moulin Rouge* in her spread in the Red journal by doing all those things, then throwing some lace and painting over her page for good measure. Can anyone possibly overdo cancan dancers?

TIPS

• For her White journal cover, Lynne Perrella layered old letters, envelopes, wisps of ivory gift papers and tissue paper. A final layer of papers was then stamped with acrylic paints. Another technique Lynne used was to paint and over-paint, then scrub the surface with a rag to expose the multiple colors that emerged. Acrylic and metallic stencils and journaling in a soft pencil were sometimes added as a final layer.

• To create her luscious and layered antique tapestry look, pattern-princess Anne Bagby often started with watercolor paper, then applied paint, gesso, stencils, stamps and stitching. She sometimes used paper punches like carving tools along the edges. For a final touch, she applied encaustic waxes or glazes.

• Monica Riffe spread thick gesso onto a page, then closed the book, transferring gesso to the opposite page. The result is a textural surface that resembles stucco and provides a base for rubbed-in color. Monica explained her use of dried acrylic paint: "I have a friend who does acrylic painting, and uses a Frisbee as her pallet. She peels off the dried paint and gives it to me. I simply tear bits with nice color blends, and 'glue' them down with gel medium. Waxed paper is also handy as a temporary pallet for acrylic paints. When it's dry, the colorful waxed paper can be used in collages."

• Judi Riesch captured the whisper of a winter forest with white vellum, paint, doilies, and feathers on a page. For another spread, she showcased white in shades from pearl to parchment, creating as many as six layers out of wedding invitations, vellum envelops, pattern pieces, lace, photographs, buttons, and tulle.

• Lisa Renner rolled a brayer over her pages with acrylic paints, then rubbed colored chalk or Rub 'n Buff over the dry paint for highlights. Spackle compound rubbed with burnt sienna or commercial crackle finish also added patina to her pages.

Notion

to Sew

All of the *True Colors* journals exhibit a cosmic co-mingling of materials, a raid on Grandma's button box and a sassy "I can sew anything on anything" attitude. Appliqués, dress patterns, elastic, buttons, lace, denim, and yes, even, a brassiere extender, found their way onto journal pages. From Keely Barham, who has worked with fabric for more than 20 years, to Anne Bagby, a novice seamstress, who tried stitching on paper with her new sewing machine, the artists used needles right along with their paint brushes

TIPS

From Keely Barham:

- Collage strips of paper together with zigzag stitching.
- Highlight quilted fabric with French knots.
- Add quotes with stem-stitch embroidery.
- Include fabric, buttons and fibers to a painted collage.
- Glue a small "art quilt" to the page.

The colors in fabric are an inspiration for Teesha Moore, who makes entire journals out of fabric and prefers to sew rather than glue items to a page.

From Teesha Moore:

- Add fabric pockets for tuck-ins.
- Sew fabric to paper, then glue to book pages.
- Age fabric with a blow pen.
- Sew a transparency over fabric.
- Color fabric with artist crayons.

Tag, You're It!

EACH THING IN THE UNIVERSE IS A VESSEL FULL TO THE BRIM WITH WISDOM AND BEAUTY.

Tags appear in every size, shape and color throughout the journals. Tiny tags added detailed accents; large tags starred as focal points. Some tags were tucked quietly into a pocket, while others shouted with a riot of trailing fibers.

TIPS

- Sew, collage and stamp on tags. Embellish with anything within reach.
- Attach leaves, appliqués, scarabs and jewelry.
- Alter tags from clothing and other merchandise.
- Note the riotous tags that rock the already rollicking Hot Pink & Orange journal.

Lisa Renner often includes metal tags to accent her wire and mesh constructions. Her suggestions:

- Use 16-gauge craft metal (copper) and cut into a tag shape.
- Hammer the letters with metal alphabet stamps. Sets come in full alphabets and are available in different sizes.
- Rub the surface with black acrylic paint to emphasize the letters.
- To make cardboard look like metal, apply Modern Options to give the surface a rusty patina. Then use the metal stamps to imprint on the cardboard.

So Transparent

The Red journal announced, up front, that acetate transparencies were red-hot with the *True Colors* artists. Many, particularly Sarah Fishburn, explored the possibilities of transferring art to a transparency. They achieved a wonderful dimensional effect by using transparencies over backgrounds and photos. With the addition of color and all manner of embellishments, these see-through sheets promise abundant inspiration for your own journal pages.

TIPS
- Add washes of metallic paint to the back of transparent images.
- Attach transparencies over fabric or metal.
- Use two transparencies together for additional depth.
- Attach transparencies to page with brads, eyelets, stars, or flowers.
- Cut images of wings from transparencies to transform just about anyone into an angel.
- Make transparencies into envelopes and tags.
- Pass transparency through the copier a second time after copying the image to add poetry or text.

A Touch of Mica

Mica is a flexible, glass-like material that comes in sheets and small, chip-sized pieces. It's a mineral that can be separated into very thin layers, and comes in clear or various colors, including pale brown, yellow, green, and black. Many of the *True Colors* artists found all kinds of uses for mica. Nina Bagley even printed words on it: "I use words on a variety of surfaces--everything from metal to paper, ribbons to rust," Nina says. Mica can be attached to a surface with brads or eyelets or slipped inside envelopes of all sizes.

TIPS
- Separate each layer of mica for varying colors.
- Write on mica with a gold pen or glue words to the surface.
- Rubber stamp on it. You can also stamp mica with embossing powder; heat guns will not harm it.
- Use foil to hold tiles together for a stained glass effect.
- Adhere art paper to back of mica.
- Cut edges with decorative scissors.
- Paint on front or back.
- Use in collage art for window effects.

Meshing

Around

Copper mesh and wire screen in art journals? But of course!

Lisa Renner constructed pockets and pages from flexible wire mesh. Nina Bagley overlaid her book's spine with fine mesh. It formed a base for the artist to attach beads, lockets, stones, and metal hearts. Ordinary wire screen made an appearance over and under photographs as an element in collages. Both the Sepia and Metallics journals feature many examples of mesh.

TIPS
- Copper mesh can be treated with chemicals or simply laid over the element on an electric stove to alter the color. Do not leave it unattended!
- Attach mesh with eyelets or brads at each corner.
- Affix mesh or screen to page with copper wire or copper tape.
- Fold mesh or screen over on itself for smooth edges.

Over the Edge

A butterfly peeks over the edge of a book; fabric flowers sprout from the top of another journal. A wisp of lace and loops of vintage ribbon invite a closer look. The color journals are tarted up and bursting at the seams with exuberant embellishments and funky items you never dreamed would adorn the pages of a book.

TIPS
- Adopt this philosophy: When it comes to art journals, anything worth doing is worth overdoing.
- Decorate pages and covers with sequins, netting, raffia, fringe, fabric, coins and beads.
- Let them all hang out!
- Overstitch page edges with metallic thread or yarn.
- Attach fabric leaves around the page.
- Coins and bells add sound.
- All types of fibers can be inserted into the spine and tied to the book.

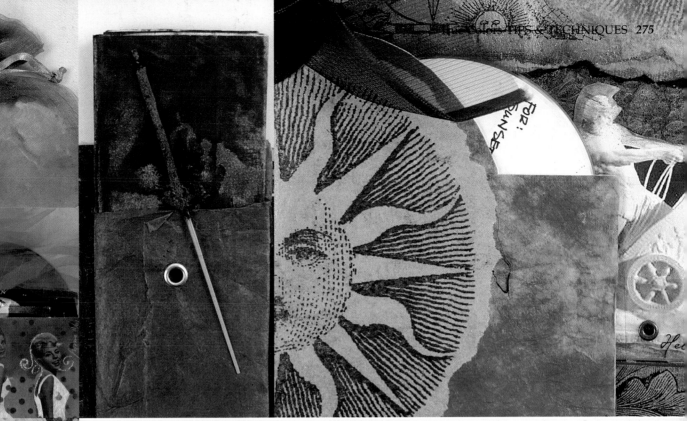

The Five Senses

A whiff of vanilla, the tinkle of a bell, the feel of vintage fabric. Who says art is only for the eyes?

On the pages of *True Colors*, you will be tempted to taste Pop Rock candy, enjoy the scent of candlewax encased in organdy and feel textures ranging from silk to rusted metal. For the ears, a CD in each journal with special titles selected by Michelle Ward adds harmony to the color themes.

TIPS
- Place incense or potpourri in an envelope and attach to the page.
- Tuck a sprig of lavender between the pages.
- Add cloves and herbs to collages.
- Apply perfume to the page edge.
- Use contrasting textures and materials; plastic and velvet, leather and feathers.
- Melt scented candlewax as part of the art.

Stamps & Threads

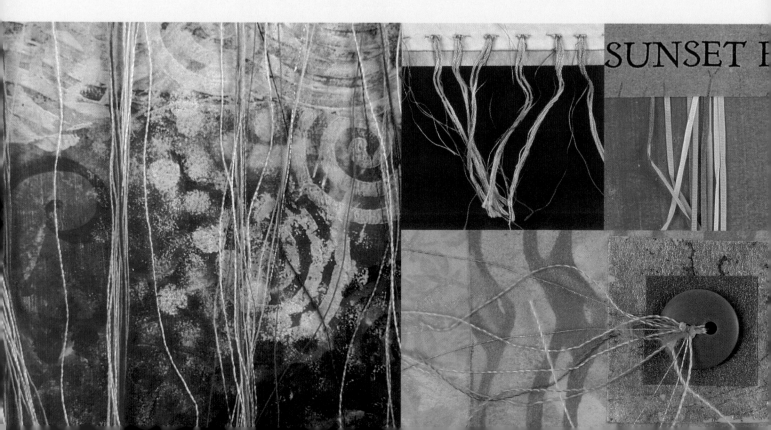

SUNSET

"If you are going to use one stamp, use them all!" Lynne Perrella says. She's only half-joking. Many of the *True Colors* artists used stamps and threads to create interesting texture on their pages.

"After layering on several techniques, I love to use stamps as tools to get to a place of color and light. I seem to search for the ones I can use for texture rather than images," says Linn Jacobs. "The process seems to be organic. Something happens and then there is a reaction and another layer is added and then--and then--and then-- and sometimes it's so hard to stop! " For her signature final touch, Linn often added layers of multicolored silk thread.

"The threads were a result of longing for a little something you could touch—almost like atmosphere. I kept thinking about that delicate haze you see at sunset, all those minuscule water droplets suspended in the air. I wanted something that would shimmer like the rays of sunlight just as it's sinking beyond the curve of the ocean, something silky and tender."

LINN JACOBS' TIP
• Start with paste paper or painted papers and over-paint, stamp, and retouch with acrylics, then use sequin scrim as a stencil for the multi-color dots.

It's My Nature

For color, design, texture and proportion, you can't top Mother Nature. Just ask Lisa Hoffman. She used so many twigs on her journal pages, they practically sprout leaves. She wrapped the twigs in everything from duct tape to felt or wound them with wire, shells, ribbon, muslin, and feathers.

On occasion, leaves literally dropped into the pages of *True Colors*. Sarah Fishburn used leaves that fell onto a page as she worked; rather than remove them, she placed them on wet paint, then rolled the page with a brayer.

All Lynne Perrella had to do was stroll through her property to gather leaves, sprigs and other greenery for her pages.

TIPS
- Affix dried flowers with matte medium.
- Preserve leaves in Microfleur from US ArtQuest.
- Press skeleton leaves into gel medium. Highlight with paint or Rub 'n Buff.
- Mount leaves on tags and tuck them in envelopes.
- Most importantly, let all the colors of nature inspire your art.

Take Cover

Whether the artists opted for a new book or an antique tome falling apart at the seams, the covers and structure of the journals were as wide-ranging as the techniques within. Lisa Hoffman was drawn to silver metal. Linn Jacobs, Keely Barham, and Teesha Moore opted for the softer look of fabric. Judi Riesch cobbled together parts from leather volumes for her Sepia journal. Some were engineering wonders; others were lashed together with wire, twine or tape. Each one became an adventure for both the artist and viewer.

TIPS

- Remove and reassemble pages from a horizontal to a vertical format.
- Add paper extensions to create foldout pages.
- Attach smaller pages to the inside binding.
- Cut pages vertically in varying widths for a "book within a book."
- Incorporate components from other books: A spine, cover or marbled end papers.
- Glue pages together for strength and for cutting out windows.
- Create the art on watercolor paper, fabric or canvas and attach to the page when finished.

Self Portraits
Meet the Artists Behind *True Colors*

Fifteen artists from around the United States participated in the *True Colors* project. Each brought her unique talent, experience and perspective to the art journals. Meet project organizer Lynne Perrella and the other women who created the amazing artwork in this book:

LYNNE PERRELLA

True Colors Organizer

Lynne Perrella is a mixed-media artist, author and graphic designer/illustrator. Her interests include collage, assemblage, one-of-a-kind books, and art journals.

She is on the editorial advisory board of two magazines, *Somerset Studio®* and *Legacy*, and makes regular contributions to *PLAY—The Art of Visual Journals*, published by Teesha Moore. Her work appears regularly in books and publications, including *Collage for the Soul: Expressing Your Hopes and Dreams Through Art* and *Altered Books, Collaborative Journals, and Other Adventures in*

Bookmaking, from Rockport, as well as *The Art & Craft of Handmade Books*, from Lark. She is also the co-author of *Artist Journals and Sketchbooks*, to be published by Rockport in March 2004, and her work will be featured in *Spirit Houses* by Carol Owen, to be published by Lark in 2004.

Lynne was part of a 19-month art doll collaboration featured in *The Art Doll Chronicles* by Stampington & Company. She exhibits collage in galleries throughout the Berkshires and was included in a group show at The New Britain Museum of American Art. She conducts creativity workshops at various venues, including ArtFest in Seattle and Carole Segal's Studio of Fine Art in Montreal, Canada. Her interest in teaching comes from "an enjoyment of sharing the creative sandbox with other kindred artists, and making mutual discoveries in a supportive and enthusiastic environment."

Lynne has owned and operated Acey Deucy Rubber Stamps for the past 15 years. Her catalog features her original illustrations and collage compositions, available as quality rubber stamps. Her interest in stamping dates back to an early and memorable encounter with *The Rubber Stamp Album*, a definitive (out-of-print) book about correspondence art. A career in corporate communications and advertising and promotion was soon shelved, as she shifted gears into the "more playful and eclectic world of rubber." She lives with her husband, John, and two orange cats in Columbia County, New York.

Contact: Lynne Perrella
P.O. Box 194, Ancram, NY 12502
Website: *www.LKPerrella.com*

ANNE BAGBY

Anne Bagby thinks of herself as a painter, but she enjoys all of the paper arts.

She moved to Tennessee more than 20 years ago and started working in oil and watercolor, but over the years her medium shifted to watercolor and acrylic. After years of creating still life paintings, she recently began considering the figure, working out compositions in journals and books, making puppets, and focusing on her drawing skills (while still working on conventional paintings).

In any medium Anne is working in, she considers herself an experimental painter. Her ambition is that her paintings be "complex, mysterious and beautiful." Whether she is using masks, layers, stamps, stencils, or collage, her intention is to continue working until the piece has the richness of a tapestry.

Her art has been featured in more than 30 one-woman shows across the United States and is displayed each November at Gallery One in Winchester, Tennessee. Anne conducts workshops introducing watercolor artists to rubber stamps and for rubber stamp artists introducing them to acrylic paint.

Contact: Anne Bagby
242 Shadowbrook Road, Winchester, TN 37398
E-mail: *annebagby@bellsouth.net*

Violet & Yellow

NINA BAGLEY

Nina Bagley is a jewelry designer and mixed-media artist from Sylva, North Carolina. For 15 years her full-time career has been transforming vintage images and words into sterling silver collage jewelry as wearable art. Her artwork has been featured in boutiques, museum shops and magazines across the United States.

Her passion for the book as art form has caused her to explore the marriage of paper and metal as interactive design. Being able to create a piece of art that truly speaks to its viewer through emotion conveyed with an image, with a word—this is what makes her work feel complete, says the artist.

When Nina isn't hammering words into silver or assembling images to paper and metal, she is wading in her river searching for river glass, teaching art workshops throughout the U.S., and spending time with her two sons, Robin and Roy, and her springer spaniel Aspen.

Contact: Nina Bagley
E-mail: *papernina@aol.com*
Website: *itsmysite.com/ninabagleydesign/*

Metallics

KEELY BARHAM

Keely Barham is a mixed-media artist from Anaheim, California. Although she likes to explore different mediums, she's primarily interested in fabric and textile art. She also enjoys beadwork.

A self-taught artist, Keely has been making things all of her life and has always liked to draw and paint. Three years ago she turned her artwork into a business by selling her creations. She teaches mixed-media workshops locally and at retreats and rubber stamp stores throughout the United States. Her work has been published in *Rubberstampmadness*, *Somerset Studio*®, and *Belle Armoire*®. She was also one of nine artists who participated in a collaboration that became the subject of a book from Stampington & Company® called *The Art Doll Chronicles*.

Keely is married and has two teenage daughters. She enjoys supporting her daughters' various activities when she's not busy in her studio.

Contact: Keely Barham
E-mail: *FabFrogDesigns@aol.com*
Website: *www.itsmysite.com/FabricFrogDesigns*

SARAH FISHBURN

Sarah Fishburn has been an artist of one kind or another for at least as long as her husband and four grown children can remember. These days, her medium is collage.

Sarah has transformed a corner of the living room in her Fort Collins, Colorado, home into an art studio. Her recent projects include pages for an annual collaborative calendar, commissioned custom collages, and an altered book project, *Unrepresented Women in the Arts*.

Sarah's art has been published in 'zines and magazines such as *ARTitude, Elements & Seasons, Home/Arts*, and *Memory Makers*, and can also be seen in several books: *Creative Paper Techniques for Scrapbooks, Creative Photo Cropping for Scrapbooks, Punch Your Art Out*, and *Quilted Scrapbooks*. She has taught classes both locally and nationally.

When she's not playing with paper, fabric, jewels, photos, and other "cool stuff," or posting the end results on her website, Sarah loves to read, travel and laugh with her family.

Contact: Sarah Fishburn
E-mail: *gerety@verinet.com* or *sarah_fishburn@yahoo.com*
Website: *www.frii.com/~gerety/SarahFishburn*

CLAUDINE HELLMUTH

Claudine Hellmuth is a nationally-known collage artist. Her work has been chosen as fine art poster designs, featured in numerous magazines, used as book cover artwork, and published as rubber stamps, drink coasters, journals, magnets, and more.

In addition to creating her artwork full-time, Claudine teaches mixed-media collage workshops in the United States and Canada. She is currently writing a book about her techniques with Northlight Books, to be published in fall/winter 2003.

With a fine arts degree from the Corcoran College of Art, Claudine approaches collage the old-fashioned way. She enjoys the challenge of working with a variety of materials, cutting, pasting and painting her artworks by hand.

Claudine's studio and home is in Orlando, Florida, where she lives with her husband, Paul, and their very spoiled four-legged children: Toby the Wonder Dog and Melvis the Cat.

Contact: Claudine Hellmuth
2457 A. South Hiawassee Road, PMB #106,
Orlando, FL 32835
E-mail: *CHellmuth@aol.com*
Website: *www.collageartist.com*

Green

LISA HOFFMAN

Lisa Hoffman currently makes her home in Fort Collins, Colorado, and is experimenting with as many mediums as she can get her hands in and on. Driven by humor and a sense of irony, her recent art-related forays have taken her into the world of assemblage and painting. Collaborative projects have kept her plate full and overflowing.

Lisa left her native East Coast and life in the jewelry business in 1979 to join her husband's Colorado rubber stamp company. She soon found herself manning the company's art supply and rubber stamp store, the art school and contract manufacturing. After her husband's death in 1989, Lisa and her husband's family retained the business, which closed its doors in 2000.

Lisa is also the co-founder of The Manifest Destiny Art Center in Boulder, Colorado. She and business partner Nancy Anderson, a jeweler and assemblage artist, offer classes, workshops and seminars that stretch the boundaries of the traditional art school. In addition, the center offers a program that works with youths at risk of drug addiction and/or in need of adult role models.

When not "caught in the act of wielding various art supplies," Lisa can be found writing poetry, prose and essays fueled by life with her partner Jim, her son Micah and her white dog sidekick, Matisse.

Contact: Lisa Hoffman
E-mail: *lisahoffman@qwest.net*

Forest Floor

LINN C. JACOBS

Linn C. Jacobs is a retired art teacher and mixed-media artist from Tacoma, Washington, who loves to "dabble" in paper, paint, beads, buttons, thread, tiny tags, and color.

For more than a decade, Linn and a friend coordinated an Art Share holiday bazaar. She has participated in other collaborations, including an art doll project organized by Catherine Moore. Recent exhibitions of her artwork include a display of her art boxes and books at the BKB Gallery in Tacoma.

Linn designed layouts and some of the graphics for a quarterly journal called *Color Trends*. The artist was also mentioned in a self-published book called *One Bead at a Time: Exploring Creativity with Bead Embroidery* by artist Robin Atkins.

Linn holds a bachelor's degree in art and art education. She has taught crafts in grade school and art classes in middle school and at the college level. She has been married for 47 years and has three children and three grandchildren.

Contact: Linn C. Jacobs
c/o BKB & Company
2701 North 21st street, Tacoma, WA 98406
(253) 620-4937
E-mail: *bkbcompany@qwest.net*
Website: *www.bkbcompany.com*

MARYLINN KELLY

Marylinn Kelly is a mixed-media artist who lives in South Pasadena, California, with her film student son, Lucas. Her work ranges from rubber stamp designs for the Rubbermoon Company to illustrated one-of-a-kind jewelry.

She has been the subject of two feature stories in *Rubberstampmadness*, for which she has also written articles. For several years, she has been a contributing writer for *The Studio Zine* and has had her color designs produced as greeting cards by Painted Hearts and Friends. She's largely self-taught as an artist.

After retiring from working as a newspaper reporter, copywriter and secretary, she had the opportunity to explore design and illustration, which she has been doing for nearly 10 years. She has always enjoyed making things with paper. "I consider myself a late bloomer and know that it is never too late to discover ourselves and our gifts," she says.

KAREN MICHEL

Karen Michel is a mixed-media artist from Long Island, New York. Her work integrates altered books, collage, painting, sculpture, photography, and art journals. For the past eight years, she has explored different ways to bring these various mediums together.

Karen studied art at the School of Visual Arts in New York City and The Institute of American Indian Arts in Santa Fe, New Mexico. She has exhibited her work both nationally and internationally. Her work has also been published in two books, *Collage for the Soul* and *The Decorated Page*.

Karen helps run Creative Art Space for Kids, Inc., the nonprofit art studio and gallery founded by her husband, artist Carlo Thertus, in Lynbrook, New York. The project's mission is to open children up to the world of art and self-expression through studio art classes and gallery exhibitions. Karen also teaches at various art events around the United States and Canada. When she's not creating art, Karen enjoys hunting seashells and collecting lost feathers.

Contact: Karen Michel
E-mail: *karen@karenmichel.com*
Website: *www.karenmichel.com* and *www.creativeartspaceforkids.org*

Violet & Green

TEESHA MOORE

Teesha Moore is a visual journal artist from Issaquah, Washington. She publishes two art magazines, *The Studio Zine* and *PLAY—The Art of Visual Journals*, and sells her work throughout the United States, primarily at rubber stamp shows.

Teesha prefers visual journaling, painting, graphic work, and textiles, but she likes to skip around between all the mediums to keep her work fresh. She is co-owner of the rubber stamp company, Zettiology. She also plans ArtFest, an annual 400-person creativity retreat in Port Townsend, Washington, as well as several smaller 30-person retreats closer to the Seattle area.

Teesha teaches journaling and journal-making classes around the country with her husband, Tracy Moore. Her work has appeared in a few magazines and books, including *Somerset Studio®*, *Making Journals by Hand* and *Rubberstampmadness*.

Contact: Teesha Moore
Alternative Arts Productions, Box 3329, Renton, WA 98056
Fax: (425) 271-5506
E-mail: *artgirl777@aol.com*
Website: *www.teeshamoore.com*

Hot Pink & Orange

LISA RENNER

Lisa Renner is a mixed-media paper and clay artist. She began using rubber stamps in 1991 and considers them to be among the most versatile tools on the market.

She enjoys working with many mediums, including paper, acrylic paints, fabric, wire, and polymer clay. She especially likes to create three-dimensional art, such as boxes, books, jewelry, and purses. A self-taught artist, she has been teaching classes both locally and nationally since 1997. Her work has been published in *The Stamper's Sampler*®, and *Somerset Studio*®, both of which honored her as a featured artist. Her work is also included in the books *Stamp Art* by Sharilyn Miller and *The Art of Paper Collage* by Susan Pickering Rothamel.

Says the artist, "During the day I work for a periodontist as a surgery coordinator, and by night I work as an artist!" Recently, she has been making cigar box purses for sale in boutiques.

Lisa lives just north of Dallas with her husband, two children, two dogs and one "conceited" cat.

Contact: Lisa Renner
E-mail: *lisarenner@attbi.com*

JUDI RIESCH

Judi Riesch is a mixed-media artist from Philadelphia, Pennsylvania, who has been working with paper and collage for more than 35 years.

Judi loves combining painting and printmaking techniques to create two- or three-dimensional pieces. She describes her work as "a kind of layering of vintage photos, trims, papers, and found objects." Her work has been shown in several galleries in Pennsylvania and the Southwest. In addition, her art has been featured in *Somerset Studio*®, *Rubberstampmadness*, *The Studio Zine*, and *PLAY—The Art of Visual Journals*, as well as several books to be published in 2003. She sells commissioned work through her company, Fragments.

Judi has a bachelor's of art degree in art education and a master's degree in media arts. She has been married to her husband, John, for 33 years, and they have two children, Jen, 30, and Christian, 25. When she is not making art, she enjoys spending time with her family and searching for continued inspiration in antique stores, flea markets and the occasional attic.

Contact: Judi Riesch
E-mail: *jjriesch@aol.com*
Website: *itsmysite.com/judiriesch*

Blue & Ochre

Sepia

MONICA RIFFE

Monica Riffe, mixed-media artist, first expressed herself in alternative media as a child, when she competed with her sister to create "the prettiest Christmas cookie" and found herself experimenting with the powdered sugar icing. Since then, she has been a professional potter, rubber stamp designer, metal smith, and assemblage artist.

A published designer, Monica has taught a wide range of art classes throughout the United States, including workshops at ArtFest in Port Townsend, Washington. Her rubber stamps, based on her hand-carved designs, have been distributed nationally. A decade of mail-art exchanges with other artists has led to a number of national and international collaborations.

Ephemera, found objects and metals are her current materials of choice, and she says she is happiest when "lost in the haphazard reverie of creating."

Monica cultivates art in Fort Collins, Colorado, along with a garden and her family: a husband, son, daughter, and two cats.

MICHELLE WARD

Michelle Ward is a designer from Piscatway, New Jersey who primarily works with paper and paint in art journals and on canvas. She's been keeping art journals for two years. She also creates dimensional assemblage art.

Michelle has been a rubber stamp artist for 10 years and began designing images for stamping six years ago. She has her own company, Green Pepper Press, which sells unmounted rubber sheets. She has created images for Stampington & Company® and Stampers Anonymous. Michelle has also taught at Artiology arts retreat and Luna Studio in New Jersey and currently hosts workshops at her studio in art journaling, bookmaking and altered books. Her artwork has been published in several magazines, including *Somerset Studio*®.

Michelle attended the University of Minnesota, receiving a bachelor's degree in Interior Architecture and Design. She also studied at the University of Birmingham, England, and the Massachusetts College of Art. After leaving the interior design field, she began working as a freelance graphic artist. Michelle has a husband, Graham, and three children: Peter, Sam and Fallon.

Contact: Michelle Ward
P.O. Box 73, Piscataway, NJ, 08855-0073
E-mail: *GRNPEP@optonline.net*
Website: *www.greenpepperpress.com* and
www.itsmysite.com/mich

Green   *Autumn*

About The Publisher

Since 1994, Stampington & Company® of Laguna Hills, Calif., has become a leading source of information and inspiration for arts and crafts lovers around the world.

Launched with a small line of rubber stamps by President/Publisher Kellene Giloff, the company has expanded to include more than 1,000 stamp images and four best-selling publications: *Somerset Studio®*, *Belle Armoire®*, *The Stampers Sampler®*, and *Stampington Inspirations™*. In 2002, Stampington unveiled *Legacy*, a quarterly magazine dedicated to creating family history art, and in May 2003 it launched *Art Doll Quarterly™*, marking yet another chapter in the company's history of innovations in the crafting industry.

Known for their outstanding color photography, these publications provide a forum for readers to share their beautiful handmade creations while gaining knowledge and ideas by seeing the works of fellow artists. Since its debut in 1997, *Somerset Studio* has become the industry standard for paper arts publications. The bi-monthly magazine attracts a large and devoted following of readers interested in the latest innovations in papercrafts, art stamping, and calligraphy.

The Stampers Sampler, the sister publication to *Somerset Studio* launched in 1994, is a bi-monthly magazine filled with hand-stamped artwork contributed by readers and accompanied by detailed sample instructions. *Stampington Inspirations* was introduced in 1999 to showcase the company's own rubber stamp images in a variety of projects, with complete instructions, templates, and full-color samples of the artwork. Launched in 2001, *Belle Armoire* has become an instant hit with art-to-wear lovers by highlighting fabric arts, creative jewelry and fashion accessories, rubber stamping, beading projects, embroidery designs and handmade garments. *Legacy* showcases all kinds of handmade artwork incorporating family history photographs, documents, and memorabilia. Elegant scrapbook pages, home décor items, journals, wearable art, paper crafts and much more are presented, and renowned genealogy experts share solid advice on researching one's family roots. Stampington's newest publication, *Art Doll Quarterly*, brings together many art forms in contemporary doll artistry.

In addition, Stampington & Company produces special publications, including: *Somerset Studio Gallery*, filled with hundreds of arts and crafts submitted by readers; *Catch Up Issue™*, showcasing hundreds of stamped samples that could not be squeezed into the regular issue of *The Stampers' Sampler*; *Holiday Extra*, featuring hand-stamped holiday artwork, and *Return to Asia*, with more than 1,000 samples of paper arts influenced by the Orient.

More information about Stampington & Company publications, along with an online shop of its extensive line of rubber stamps, art-related gifts, and unique handcrafting essentials, can be found on the Web at *www.stampington.com*. Whether reaching people online or through one of its beautiful print publications, the company remains dedicated to nurturing creative minds and spirits.

Stampington & Company®

22992 Mill Creek, Suite B
Laguna Hills CA 92653
Phone: (949) 380-7318
U.S. toll-free: 877-STAMPER
Fax: (949) 380-9355

www.stampington.com